WITHDRAWN

Zones of Strain

Zones of Strain.
A Memoir of the Early Cold War

Alfred Connor Bowman

Hoover Institution Press
Stanford University, Stanford, California

The Hoover Institution on War, Revolution and Peace, founded at Stanford University in 1919 by the late President Herbert Hoover, is an interdisciplinary research center for advanced study on domestic and international affairs in the twentieth century. The views expressed in its publications are entirely those of the authors and do not necessarily reflect the views of the staff, officers, or Board of Overseers of the Hoover Institution.

Library of Congress Cataloging in Publication Data

Bowman, Alfred Connor, 1904–
Zones of strain.

(Hoover Press publication; 273)
Bibliography: p.
Includes index.
1. Friuli-Venezia Giulia (Italy)—Politics and government.
2. Italy—History—Allied occupation, 1943–1947.
3. Military government—Italy—Friuli-Venezia-Giulia.
4. Trieste (Italy)—Politics and government.
5. Bowman, Alfred Connor, 1904–
6. Friuli-Venezia Giulia (Italy)—Governors—Biography.
7. Allied Military Government—Biography.
I. Title.
DG975.F855B68   1982   945'.39   82–11700
ISBN 0–8179–7731–7

Hoover Press Publication 273

© 1982 by the Board of Trustees of the
Leland Stanford Junior University
All rights reserved
Printed in the United States of America

Design by P. Kelley Baker

Permission to reprint the Appendix, *Report on Local Government Organization in Venezia Giulia*, granted by the author, Ralph R. Temple, J.D., PH.D.

To the dedicated men and women of many nationalities who helped hold the Cold War at the lukewarm level at the southern end of the Iron Curtain following World War II

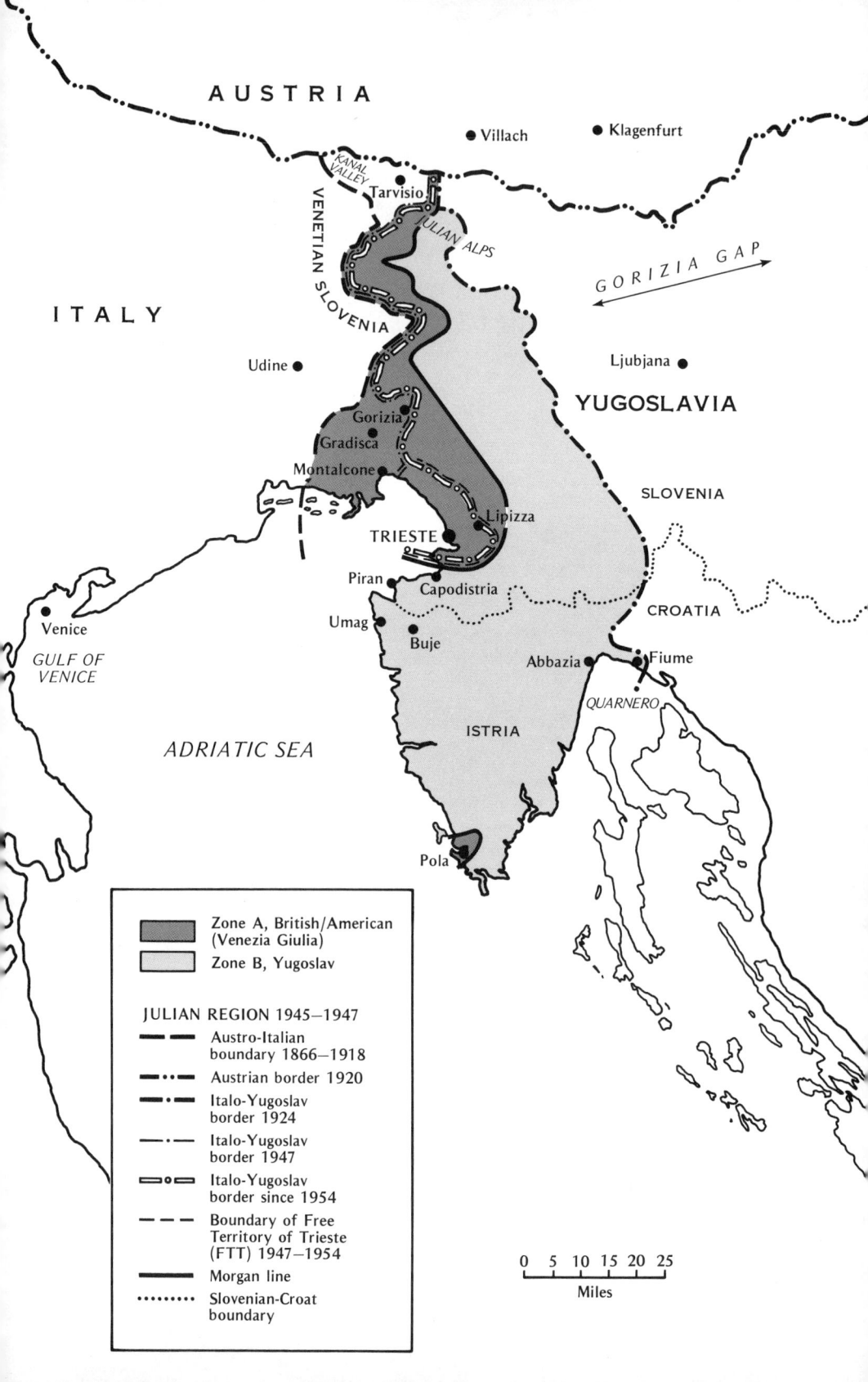

Contents

Foreword ix
Acknowledgments xi
Introduction 1
Military Government and the Cold War 6
Winter on the Gothic Line 13
Partisans 23
Confrontation of Allies 39
The Domain 43
Summer 1945 52
My Days and Evenings 66
Rank, Mistresses, and the Press 75
Government and Schools 91
Prelude to Decision 101
The Home Stretch 114
Arrivederci, Bowman 127
Czech Interlude 143
Retrospect and Prospect 151
Appendix 159
Bibliography 163
Chronology 165
Index 169
About the Author 177

I could recall the hours and days and months on end in which my associates, principally [John] Foster Dulles, and I, had focused our concern . . . on such things as a tiny patch of land at the head of the Adriatic . . . On these bits of geography and the handfuls of people within them in those years, war and peace at times could have hung in the balance.

Dwight D. Eisenhower
Mandate for Change 1953–1956, pp. 574–75

Foreword

The people of Trieste loved the New Zealand boys

Having been in command of the British and American troops in Venezia Giulia in the two years following the end of the Second World War and thus having worked in close association with Colonel Bowman, I count it a pleasure and privilege to comment on his book, containing as it does the story of his problems and experiences as head of the Allied Military Government of that region at a critical time in its history.

When the allied troops and the Yugoslav Partisans met in Trieste at the end of the war, that city and the surrounding territory became a powder keg in which a spark could have set off an explosion with serious international consequences, and possibly an outbreak of hostilities in Europe between East and West. That this did not happen was due to the tact and diplomacy with which the situation was handled, and to a considerable measure of patience and restraint on all sides. This was a remarkable achievement, and Colonel Bowman, who had responsibility for the administration of local government, played a unique and outstanding part in it.

As Bowman's story unfolds, the reader will appreciate the firm yet fair and tactful way in which the author discharged his varied and often difficult and dangerous responsibilities, his patience and good humor in the face of provocation, the careful thought and wisdom he brought to bear on problems demanding his decision, his human understanding, and his policy of give and take, in his dealings with Slavs, Latins, and allies alike.

This book will be of the greatest interest not only to historians and those who were directly involved in the problems it covers, but to the general reading public as well. The situation in Venezia Giulia at the end of the Second World War was not dissimilar to the situation in other parts of the world where there were conflicting aspirations and fears, for example, in Cyprus where, ten years later, as governor of a British colony inhabited by people of two other ethnic groups—this time Greeks and Turks—I had to deal with some very similar problems.

Though his conclusions in regard to the final settlement of the Trieste problem are open to argument, and despite some understandable nostalgic sentiment, there is much in Colonel Bowman's story to be learned by those involved in international problems now and in the future. Finally, it may not be irrelevant to add that professional military commanders and staff officers are not always as inept at handling such problems as the media of today would often have their readers and listeners believe.

Field Marshal Lord Harding of Petherton

Acknowledgments

The author and his family in the garden of the family quarters on the Venice Lido, summer 1946

That I must one day, as a matter of duty, undertake the writing of this memoir was first made clear to me many years ago by Dr. Thomas G. Bergin, now professor emeritus of Romance Languages at Yale University, who had been a senior staff officer of the Allied Commission (for Italy) during and immediately following World War II. Since I produced my first tentative draft manuscript several years ago, my most indefatigable source of inspiration and furnisher of services has unquestionably been my agent, Matie Molinaro who, as a member of the Allied Information Service staff, had been a direct participant in many of the events here chronicled. Her husband, Dr. Giulio Molinaro of the Department of Italian Studies of the University of Toronto, also "present at the Creation," has provided not only occasional memory refreshment, but informed guidance concerning matters of Italian history and culture.

In the later stages of my book's gestation, Dr. Bogdan C. Novak of the Department of History of the University of Toledo, who had served as an educator in Venezia Giulia during my time there, has been an untiring and generous guide to the historical backgrounds of the areas in which the events of my story took place. Following acceptance of my manuscript by Hoover Institution, Dr. Milorad Drachkovitch, senior fellow and archivist of the Institution, has been of very great assistance in helping to smooth out its last rough edges and getting it into the editorial process.

I have relied heavily for documentary confirmation of events otherwise only dimly remembered on Dr. Ralph Temple, former deputy director of the Local Government Section of the Allied Commission and distinguished president emeritus of the Military Government Association. Professional writers Cate (Mrs. S. L. A.) Marshall, Cordelle Ballard, and Charlotte Munger carefully read my manuscript in an early stage of its development and contributed many helpful suggestions. Rachelle Marshall's editorial skills contributed greatly to the final manuscript, and Phyllis Cairns, publications manager of Hoover Institution Press, ably guided it to final publication.

Introduction

Officers of Emilia Region assembled at the author's billet, the Villa Gazzone at Bologna, to celebrate the first anniversary of the activation of the region

Although many of the events recounted in the following chapters occurred in other places, unquestionably the principal geographical focus will be on the city of Trieste—the great port city on the northeastern shore of the Adriatic in the area that the Italians now refer to as Venezia Giulia and Friuli. It was the seat of the Allied Military Government (AMG) of the British-American zone (Zone A) of the then-disputed area, which I headed from mid-1945 to mid-1947.

Venezia is simply the Italian way of spelling and pronouncing the name of the place we English-speakers call Venice. Giulia is the Italian equivalent of Julia—not a female name but an adjective connoting association with the Roman Empire of Julius Caesar. To the average American or European, Venice is most likely to evoke mind-pictures of canals, gondolas, and cathedrals, even though he or she has been taught that during the middle of this millennium Venice was almost an empire, extending over large areas of today's Italy as well as other more distant places.

Actually, the toponym Venezia Giulia did not come into general use until the latter part of the nineteenth century. Scholars credit its invention and promulgation as designation of the northeastern part of then newly united Italy to glossologist Graziado Ascoli of Gorizia. He argued that the designation of the area as Venezia was justified by the fact that the residents of the newly acquired lands spoke the same dialect as the proper Venetians. As to Giulia, he pointed out that many of the place-names of the area included Iulia or a recognizable part or corruption thereof.

He had a point. There were indeed such place-names as Forum Iulii (now Cividale) in the Friuli area (whose own name was a contraction of the Latin Forum Iulii); Iulia Parentium, now Parenzo; and Iulia Emona, the present-day Yugoslav city of Ljubljana in Slovenia. The people in the region were commonly called Foroiuliani. Historically, various writers had referred to the territory as Terra Iulia or Regionem Iuliani, and even today almost every educated person has heard of the Julian Alps.

Without questioning either Dr. Ascoli's motives or his scholarship, it should be noted that, by associating Venezia Giulia with the Roman Empire of Julius Caesar and his imperial Julian family his ideas were bound to, and did, find great favor in Italy at a time when it was crucially involved in becoming a united nation. Enthusiastic nationalists had originated the concept of irredentism—the idea that certain areas either geographically adjacent to or culturally associated with the new Kingdom of Italy, but not part of it, were unredeemed, that is, belonged to the new nation by right of history and a sort of Manifest Destiny, yet regrettably were not a part of it politically.

The irredentist concept was applied for various purposes and at various times to many different peoples and places, including the French city Nice, the islands of Corsica and Malta, and the border areas of Switzerland and Austria-Hungary. However, its principal targets were the areas and communities on the north and east shores of the Adriatic, where ethnically Italian merchants, fishermen, and settlers of all types had been living and working for centuries. It was only natural that Italian nationalists, committed to irredentist doctrine, should eagerly grasp Dr. Ascoli's thesis and exploit it to the limit.

However, despite the long association of Venezia Giulia with ethnic Italianity, the historical fact was that, after almost two millennia of being contended for by Romans, Goths, Lombards, Byzantines, Carolingian Franks, and Venetians, and by France, Austria, Italy, Germany, and the nations that now make up Yugoslavia, the northern part of the region had been a fief of Hapsburg Austria-Hungary for four hundred years. Trieste and Istria had been subject to the same suzerainty for a hundred years before they were ceded to Italy in 1918 as part of her reward for having joined the right side in World War I.

One of the most ethnically significant developments of the first millennium of the Christian era had been the incursion into the northern part of the region, beginning early in the seventh century, of Slavic tribes who dominated that area for two hundred years, later penetrating further south to become the ancestors of several of the ethnic groups that constitute today's Yugoslavia.

The city of Trieste, where I observed and intimately participated in some of the more recent and critical phases of Venezia Giulia's history, was already a prosperous fishing village when the Romans conquered the area about 178 B.C. Tergeste (the Latin version of its name) was fortified by Augustus. Thereafter, although it was never a political capital, Trieste was always the most important center of population and trade of the area east of Venice, and shared the fortunes and vicissitudes of the rest of the region for the next thousand years.

The reader will encounter other bits and pieces of the history of Trieste and its environs during its second millennium in subsequent chapters. For purposes of this introduction, therefore, I will skip over eight centuries of the city's and region's histories and resume my outline in the early nineteenth century, when the area reverted to Austria-Hungary following the defeat of Napoleon and the end of his empire.

Viewed in perspective, the nineteenth century was Trieste's real heyday. The fourth decade saw the founding, with headquarters in Trieste, of the Lloyd Triestino shipping line and of two great insurance companies—the Assicurazioni Generali and the

Riunione Adriatica di Sicurtà—which soon resulted in the city's becoming one of Europe's greatest insurance centers. Other major contributions to the city's prosperity and prestige during the half-century preceding World War I included the construction of first-rate facilities connecting the city to Vienna and other places in central Europe, the opening of the Suez Canal, and the development of steam navigation.

All these factors and influences combined to encourage and facilitate the enlargement and modernization of the port of Trieste. By 1905 the port had surpassed its great regional rival, Venice, in tonnage handled, and had become the fifth in importance in Europe, surpassed only by Hamburg, Antwerp, Genoa, and Marseilles. The city's population increased from 80,000 in 1845 to 247,099 in 1913. This was only about five thousand less than that of the city I entered and made my headquarters 32 years later.

Meanwhile, by 1870 the unification of all continental Italian-speaking peoples and their territories into a single Kingdom of Italy had been completed except for Trieste, Trento, and a few isolated communities such as Fiume and Zara on the Adriatic's eastern shore. The Italian irredentist urge to incorporate these remaining pockets of Italianity into the mother country brought Italy into World War I on the side of the Entente Allies after the secret Treaty of London, signed April 15, 1915, promised post-victory delivery of most of these communities.

This treaty, by which Great Britain, France, and Russia undertook to deliver to Italy the South Tyrol, the county of Gorizia (Görz), the Istrian peninsula, and parts of Dalmatia, was duly honored following the war. Meanwhile, however, with the breakup of the Austro-Hungarian Empire, a new state had come into being on the eastern shore of the Adriatic: Yugoslavia, the kingdom of the Serbs, Croats, and Slovenes. No sooner was it born than it began to question and contest Italy's claimed prerogatives and title to the lands we have been discussing, particularly Venezia Giulia.

After long negotiation of the conflicting claims of Italy and Yugoslavia, the treaties of St. Germain (November 10, 1919) and Rapallo (November 12, 1920) ceded Venezia Giulia and Zara to Italy, but not Fiume (Rijeka). Later, following the theatrical expedition and coup d'etat of the soldier-poet Gabriele D'Annunzio and his band of "legionaries" (which took place even while the negotiations at St. Germain were in progress), Fiume was also subjected to Italian rule by the Treaty of Rome, signed on January 17, 1924.

The ensuing quarter-century of recognized Italian sovereignty over Venezia Giulia ended when Italy, this time having chosen the wrong side in another war, surrendered to the Allied forces on September 8, 1943. Following Italy's surrender, the Germans controlled the city and the area until 1945, presumably intending to absorb it into the Greater Reich. This brings us to the beginning of the story I have set out to tell.

In the telling, I ask the tolerance and indulgence of ethnically sensitive readers in the matter of place names. In general, I have felt it appropriate and most practical to apply to the towns and geographical subdivisions of the area the place-names we actually used at the time of the events. In most cases these were the Italian toponyms, familiar to all on my team, as well as to the local population conditioned to a quarter-century of Italian rule. They were also more easily pronounced than the Slovene counterparts, which were often composed entirely of consonants (for instance, Trst for Trieste). My use of these names, some 35 years later, reflects no ethnic or national bias.

Military Government and the Cold War

Exhorting partisans to turn in their weapons

"A shadow has fallen upon the scenes so lately lighted by the Allied victory," said Winston Churchill at Westminster College in Missouri on March 5, 1946. "From Stettin in the Baltic to Trieste in the Adriatic, an Iron Curtain has descended across the continent. Behind that line lie all the capitals of the ancient states of Central and Eastern Europe."

The historic words of the greatest national leader and statesman of our century in effect amounted to a declaration that a state of war existed with its battle front along the line described. The continuing confrontation between the United States and the Union of Soviet Socialist Republics, and the adoption by each of them of various economic, political, and military expedients even to the present time, has been no less real because it involved few or no guns or bombs. We called it the Cold War.

If this was a war, it may be asked, where was its opening, partially decisive, engagement—the first show of belligerent intent by the aggressor, whose defeat in this gunless, bombless Marne or Stalingrad made its ultimate victory much more difficult, if not impossible? I assert without equivocation that this engagement occurred in Italy's Po Valley and in the North Adriatic Littoral during the biennium following the German surrender in 1945. I further suggest that its focal point as an element of the Cold War was the political and doctrinal confrontation at Trieste to which most of this book is devoted.

In order to put this subject into perspective, I found it necessary to include in my account some events involving U.S./British military government structures and procedures during and following World War II in the part of the world where Trieste is located, and this in turn requires that I define the words "military government" as I shall use them. To me, as a professional in the field, they have a precise technical significance; but I have learned during the past thirty-five years that this is not true among the American populace generally. The term has been corrupted by indiscriminate application to any totalitarian regime headed by a military person, such as the present and recent governments in such South American countries as Brazil, Peru, Chile, and Argentina.

This book has nothing to do with that type of regime. The military government concerned in the events I shall describe is a necessary function in any military operation, whether planned or not, but of course performed better when planned for. It is an integral part of war in one respect and of the aftermath of war in another. It is as old as war itself.

During the fighting, military government is the business of managing the civilian populations of areas in which the fighting forces operate, so as to (1) prevent interference with military operations; (2) promote the security and well-being of the troops; and (3) utilize local manpower, supplies and facilities, so far as is consistent with international law, to support the military effort—that is, win the war.

There are two approaches to this function, the negative and the positive. The negative, which has sometimes been too prevalent in military thinking, concentrates on keeping the people out of the way of the fighting troops, in other words, holding them down. The application of this approach lost two wars for the Germans in this century. Morality aside, it wastes military personnel who should be fighting, not policing.

The positive approach enables the military government to contribute most effectively. While it is unlikely today that military forces in any overseas war would be able to live off the land in the manner of Sherman in Georgia, the effective exploitation by military government of local resources can greatly reduce the logistical burden, and thus expedite the march to victory. In Italy, for example, early attention to the hemp-cultivation potential of land near Naples kept the Royal Navy supplied with its cables and rope in the latter days of the war. The prompt draining of sea-flooded, grain-growing areas along the lower Po River, before the salt could ruin the land, avoided the necessity of sending many extra ship-loads of grain across the Atlantic to feed starving Italians. The hiring of local labor and contractors for the repair and expansion of civilian factories, generating plants, and the like, freed highly trained combat engineers for work of more direct military consequence. This is the prime function of military government during the fighting.

After the war, a military government organization may be used, as it was in Trieste and its environs during my time there, for a different, but no less important, purpose. In the case of Trieste, two nations claimed the land. Which one was to get it, and on what terms, could not be determined until after a peace conference. Meanwhile, someone had to be in charge for the specific purposes of feeding, clothing, and housing the people, maintaining public order, and preventing disease and unrest (in short, to maintain the status quo, or something close to it) until the fate of the territory could be determined.

These are the connotations of the words "military government" as they will be used in this book. It should be added that, within any military government so defined, at any level, the exercise of power by the military governor is virtually unlimited except by orders of higher authority and the laws and customs of war. The persons governed have no rights as that word is understood under any of the constitutional systems of western countries. There is no right to vote or to speak without restraint, to bear arms, or to appeal to courts for relief from onerous action by the executive (military governor) other than by his tolerance, which must depend on conditions. The only restraints on the actions of the man who holds the job I held in Trieste are those imposed by military superiors or governments.

With some notable exceptions, the typical American Military Government officer of World War II was basically a civilian in uniform. In some circumstances, career Army people found him difficult to understand and sometimes asked why he should be there at all. For a time before I became a regional commissioner, it was my job to sell the necessity of his presence to various combat and logistical elements of British and French units, as well as our own. It was not easy. The ultimate fact is that he was selected for the duties he performed precisely because as a civilian he was deemed better qualified by experience and personal outlook to direct the process, under trained professional military supervision, of exploiting the local resources of occupied areas in support of the combat effort.

In the special case of Italy from late 1943 to mid-1945, there were two principal respects in which the military government pattern differed from that applied elsewhere. One of these was the concept of total Allied integration, rather than separate zones. The task, rather than the conquered territory, was divided—unlike the plans of administration employed in Austria and Germany. Despite the frequent use of the word "integration" in connection with military organizations during the past several decades, in a sense that had nothing to do with skin color, I believe it to be true that AMG units and operations in Italy represented its only complete application on the working level, as applied to soldiers of differing nationalities but coequal status.

All our units were mixed British-American. British commanders had American deputies, and vice versa. If a town seemed to require two officers to run and control it, one would be American and the other might be British, Canadian, Palestinian, South African, or, rarely, French; and the soldiers would also be a mixed group. Only in Italy did military government officers of all participating Allied nationalities carry on the operational job shoulder to shoulder, from the national capital down to the farm village, maintaining a unified occupied nation and at the same time learning to live, work, plan with, and learn from one another.

The other special factor was the concept of cobelligerency, and the Allied policy of building up and entrusting power as early as possible, even during actual hostilities, to the Italian government.

"Cobelligerent" was used by the British and U.S. governments to describe the ongoing relationship with Italy—late partner of Germany as one of the enemy Axis nations, but now on our side. "Ally" would have been too strong a word, tarring Italy with the turncoat brush that everyone wished to avoid as far as possible. Whether or not it was effective for the purpose is beside the point. Some distinction, it was said, had to be made between Italy and the nations that had been on our side from the beginning. The entire Italian government at that time consisted of Marshal Badoglio and a stenographer hidden away in Brindisi.

The special situation created by these factors did not exist in other theaters and called for a special method suited to the geographical, political, and tactical needs of the Italian campaign.

All of Italy, including Sicily and Sardinia, was divided into regions, whose boundaries, except for certain later consolidations for administrative reasons, corresponded roughly to the *compartimenti* or groups of provinces with historic, familiar names: Sardinia, Sicily, Calabria, Puglia, Lucania, Campania, Lazio, Umbria, Abruzzi e Molise, Marche, Tuscany, Liguria, Emilia, Piedmont, Lombardy, and Tre Venezie—"the three Venices"—Tridentina, Euganea, and Giulia. Part of the compartimento Puglia, in the heel and southeastern part of the peninsula, was a special case and from the beginning was not subject to Allied military administration, but was entrusted to the Italian government as King's Italy.

At that time, these compartimenti did not represent governmental units of Italy. Mussolini's chain of command had run from Rome to each of the provinces, without the interposition of any intermediate echelon. They were rather eclectic areas. Some maintained the boundaries of ancient kingdoms, some were united by a common culture, and others were not united at all (as we found out).

The decision to use these ancient kingdoms and dukedoms as governmental units for military government purposes was the occasion for some controversy, not only on the command and diplomatic level, but in the School of Military Government at Charlottesville, Virginia, where one crusty old regular army instructor asked rhetorically, "If Mussolini could do it [govern each of the provinces of Italy directly through prefects appointed from Rome] why can't we?" In view of this skepticism, it is of particular interest and some satisfaction to those who supported and played parts in the regional scheme, that a quarter century later, in June 1970, the electorate of Italy voted to adopt the scheme—in almost exactly the form in which we used it—as a part of the permanent governmental administrative framework of the Italian republic.

In any event, for each of these regions there was provided a team of civil affairs officers and men, in number as nearly as possible half British and half American, headed by an officer of one of these nationalities. His deputy, of the other nationality, commanded the detachment of personnel from his army who made up half of the team. The teams ranged in size from about one hundred twenty-five to one hundred fifty officers, with about the same or a somewhat greater number of British and American enlisted men. They were assembled and trained in the rear and made ready either in skeleton crews or in complete units to move forward as the areas for which they were destined were liberated.

In addition, each of the two armies in Italy—the American Fifth and the British Eighth—had its own spearhead team of AMG officers whose function was to enter the individual communes immediately behind the troops, render what first aid they could, and then turn over command to the regional team as the army moved forward. The Fifth Army team was commanded by Brig. Gen. Edgar Erskine Hume, USA, and the Eighth Army team by Group Capt. (later Air Commodore) C. E. Benson, RAF.

All of these teams and regions were supervised in all technical matters and the application of overall occupation policy by the Allied Commission in Rome, which was totally British-American integrated and directed by Chief Commissioner Adm. Ellery W. Stone, USNR, who also held the title of chief civil affairs officer on the staff of the supreme allied commander.

As operations tapered off in the rear, occupied areas became farther and farther removed from the actual battle; and as basic rehabilitation was completed, administration was turned over to the Italian government, the seat of which was moved forward from time to time until it reached Rome.

Such was the pattern that was impressed on Italy as the war progressed. With a little goodwill on all sides (and there is probably more of that in the middle of a war than under any other conditions) it worked well, except in Venezia Giulia.

Sometimes large areas of Italy remained subject to the control for AMG purposes of the combat armies (Fifth U.S. Army to the West; Eighth British Army on the Adriatic side) for long periods of time. This was particularly true from the summer of 1944 until the final movement forward in April 1945, during which period a great and important part of Italy was administered by Fifth Army AMG from a headquarters near Florence. In such circumstances, the personnel of the permanent regional teams were moved forward to positions south of their assigned areas and integrated operationally into the Army AMG units ahead of them.

In the case of the three provinces of Emilia Region on the Adriatic side in the British Eighth Army area, there was another special factor. The British element and personnel of the British Eighth Army AMG had been apprised that it would form the nucleus of the spearhead military government team for Austria where, it was then assumed, there were still battles to be fought and territory to be subjected to military government. Further, Air Commodore Benson, its chief, was designated to take charge of organization and training for this future mission.

The training area for the Austrian AMG team was to be in the vicinity of Naples, far from the current British Eighth Army operational area. It would obviously not be operationally practical for the Air Commodore to try to straddle the distance between the geographical locations of the two critical jobs. He asked me to take over his job in addition to my other duties, before it officially became mine. I agreed on the understanding that I might delegate the direction of day-to-day operations to my deputy, so that I might be free to keep in touch with the elements of my team located outside the Eighth Army area.

Winter on the Gothic Line

The author riding with his aide, unarmed and unguarded, through Slovene-inhabited suburbs of Trieste

By February 1945, I had been in Italy for about fifteen months and, due to some very favorable circumstances, had advanced in my temporary profession more rapidly than some of my associates. As regional commissioner for the Emilia-Romagna region of Italy, I was one of the Barons of the North in charge on paper of eight provinces located between the crest of the Apennines and the Po River. I say "on paper" because by that time I was actually in effective control only of three provinces on the shores of the Adriatic at the eastern end of what the world press was then referring to as the Gothic Line.

I have never learned for certain, nor have any of the many eminent scholars consulted in the preparation of this memoir been able to tell me, whether this designation alluded to the fall of Rome to the Visigoths in 410 A.D., or to Ostrogoth activities a century later, or to neither or both. So far as I know, the phrase was coined locally or by the American press in late 1944 to describe the static front, also sometimes called the Pisa-Rimini Line, where the British Eighth and the American Fifth Armies were bogged down in the Apennine snow along a line that stretched from Pisa on the Tyrrhenian Sea to the resort area of Rimini on the Adriatic.

Incredible as it seems to me in retrospect, and I am sure will appear to the reader, we had been dubbed the D-Day Dodgers by some elements of the press. The implication was that we were cowering in the Apennines in order to avoid the presumed greater hazards to life and limb of participating in the Normandy landings and the "real" war in western Europe. This was a cruel calumny indeed on the fighting troops dying every day not only in combat but from exposure and all the physical ills it can engender. The press never coined a less appropriate or more callous phrase to apply to a worthier or more valiant body of men. The officers and men in my military specialty in general did not suffer much, but it was certainly not a time of comfort, ease, and daily trips to the PX.

Be all this as it may, in early April 1945 we were still hung up on this Gothic or Pisa-Rimini Line, but hoping soon to break through the mountains and advance to Bologna, Milan, and beyond. Bologna was my special personal destination. I was to be regional commissioner (military governor) of the southern half of the Po Valley. I was already administering most of the three eastern provinces (Forli, Ravenna, and Ferrara), which the Eighth Army had taken before the rains came.

Bologna was the historic capital of the region, centered geographically in it, and the logical place from which to conduct the civil administration.

During this long winter stalemate on the Gothic or Pisa-Rimini Line, Italy south of the combat army areas was pretty well processed and as soon as the armies moved over the Apennines everything south of those mountains was ready for the Italian government. Except for Livorno (Leghorn), the American port of supply, and Ancona, which fulfilled the same function for the British, it had no further direct interest for the Allied armies. Attention was concentrated rather on the regions north of the Apennines: the "real" Italy, the breadbasket and the workshop;

the regions of Liguria, Piedmont, Lombardy, Emilia, and Tre Venezie—the Three Venices.

At the heads of three regional teams were American officers Col. Robert Marshall, New York businessman, for Piedmont; Col. Charles Poletti, ex-governor of New York, for Lombardy; and I myself for Emilia, anomalously both the richest region agriculturally and the focal center of partisan and communist activity, sometimes referred to by the press as the Kremlin of Italy.

One special feature of my region, dubbed Emilia by the Allied Commission but actually comprising both of the historic areas of Emilia and Romagna, was the existence within its boundaries of a proud and highly self-conscious independent nation—the Republic of San Marino. It was and is the oldest republic in the world, dating from 300 A.D. The Germans had treated it like the rest of the Italian boot. We obviously could not and did not want to.

I had been tremendously impressed by the proud spirit of independence and unwillingness to be beholden exhibited by the members of the Sammarinese government when I had encountered them on our entry into the republic the preceding September. I quote verbatim from my diary entry of September 21, 1944:

> We asked them what they needed, and their reply indicated that the processing and care of eighty thousand refugees who they said have entered San Marino has been handled very efficiently. They amazed us by asking for only one vehicle to assist in delivering supplies from the City of San Marino to the countryside. We had already allocated thirteen loaded trucks, and expected to need a hundred. They refused all but one. We compromised by sending only the thirteen already allocated. They said they needed no money. One gets the impression ... that these people are genuine democrats, honestly relieved at the disappearance not only of the Tedeschi but of the fascist ideology, so foreign to their national tradition, yet so forced upon them by their special geographical position. I find that I am apparently the first American officer or enlisted man to enter San Marino during this war.

Despite the brave words and admirable attitudes of its political leaders, the fact remained that Italy was the republic's major source of supply for virtually all subsistence supplies, and its only source for many, so it was my responsibility to feed and provision it during the long winter of 1944–1945.

For this purpose, I established a one-man liaison office in the capital city at the top of Mount Titano and visited the place frequently. With an area of about thirty-two square miles and fewer than 17,000 resident nationals, the little state took pride in all the accoutrements and ceremonials of any sovereign state. Its legislature, the Sovereign Grand Council, comprised sixty members from whom two were elected and inaugurated as captains regent (the executive heads of government) every six months—four each year. During a thirty-year career in public life, any citizen who wished the honor had one hundred and twenty chances to become head of state! We had the opportunity to attend one of the inaugurations, and no nation on earth could have handled the ceremony with greater finesse and dignity. On the whole, San Marino gave us no trouble, but was a focal point of tourist-type interest throughout the time that my headquarters was located only eighteen miles away.

Liguria, the smallest of the northern regions, comprising the four provinces of the Italian Riveria, was to be governed by Brig. John Matthew Carr of the British army, and the three Venices, constituting by far the largest of the regions, were apportioned to Brig. John K. Dunlop, also British. Easternmost of the Venices was Venezia Giulia, Italy's reward for her services in the First World War. This was Italia Irredenta—Italy unredeemed—background of the drama to follow.

Of course, some discretion was exercised. If the military government job coming up had to be carried out in an area being taken over by an American force, it was considered good judgment to designate an American commissioner, who could more readily communicate with commanding generals who might not be totally sold on integration. Since the mission of pacifying and occupying northwest Italy was, in the first instance, to be a responsibility of the American IV Corps under Gen. Willis D. Crittenberger, it was no coincidence that three of the four of us who attended a meeting in Rome were Americans. Although I was involved in this operation only to the extent of the westernmost three (of my total of eight) provinces that were nearest Milan, this was the reason I was in Rome on April 9, 1945.

The next morning we four "barons" flew to Florence where we were briefed by Generals Mark Clark and Al Gruenther. Later, we motorcaded to Lucca and heard from General Crittenberger. They laid out the red carpet for us colonels and the brigadier, and we enjoyed being treated like VIPs by all that brass. We were back in Rome by dinner time.

That evening, also in Rome, Duane Freese, my executive officer, was shot in the back of the neck as he taxied back to his hotel following an evening at the officers' club. He would recover, but since he was my right arm, this was a bad break—the more so since we knew the time when full operational effectiveness would be essential was only days ahead.

Two days later, on Friday the thirteenth, President Franklin D. Roosevelt died.

During the next seven days, I zigzagged around Florence, the Arno, and the lower slopes of the Apennines checking on the teams I had deployed—each south of the province it was designated to administer when things opened up. I returned to my headquarters in Riccione on April 18. The president of the Allied Commission arrived the following day. His name was Harold Macmillan, and twelve years later he would be prime minister of Great Britain.

I should say that this town of Riccione, where I had established my main headquarters for the winter, had been a summer resort before the war, and has long since reverted to that condition. My officers and I lived in a big stone house called the Villa Piva, which had recently been vacated by Field Marshal Albert Kesselring of the Wehrmacht. It was situated directly on the beach, which would have been nice for time off except that we did not arrive there until mid-September and left in April. Even so, my British deputy, Hubert Horton-Smith Hartley (Coldstream Guardsman, Eton housemaster, and former stroke on a championship Cambridge crew) used to swim eastward out of sight every day until one day in midwinter when I noticed that he didn't. Asked why, he replied: "Colonel, I started to, but found that today the pain would have exceeded the pleasure." You can't fault the logic. Hubert was a true Cantabridgian.

This was the time and milieu in which scrounging became a necessity and a fine art. British and Americans alike, in the northeast corner of the part of Italy we had wrested from the Germans, were far from normal sources of supply. We drew rations from either British or American sources when we had access to them, and also lived off the country to a degree, particularly as regards a pasta food supplement. Emilia is the pasta capital of the world's number one pasta-eating nation.

In the Emilia Region AMG milieu, the word "scrounge" achieved a prominent place in day-to-day social intercourse, as well as in official business. It was applied originally to the procurement of motor transport, which was hard to come by through official procurement channels. Not unreasonably, higher authority faced with the decision whether to allot a single available jeep to a combat unit or to AMG would generally take the former course. For the most part, we were to supply our needs in the localities in which we worked.

In each region, and in many smaller units in the field, individuals with special talent and liking for the work were relieved from other duties to enable them to devote their full time to this special aspect of the procurement process, and they soon became highly skilled. Very serviceable automobiles were found under haystacks, in the basements of houses, and buried in pits. Nor was the process confined to motor transport. Operational needs often required resort to unconventional expedients. A Red Cross disaster-relief worker personally removed the glass from the frames of a number of pictures in the local art museum of one of the villages and cut it into small panes to replace some of those smashed by German bombs in school buildings. The successful, imaginative, and discriminating scrounger became a folk hero, first class.

On April 21, the day after his arrival, I showed Mr. Macmillan around the three provinces we already had under administration. One of them was Ravenna, with Dante's tomb and its many temples, monuments, frescoes, and mosaics already in the process of repair under AMG sponsorship. There were other projects: rebuilding towns, reclaiming agricultural land flooded by the Germans with salt water, mine detecting and removal, repairing and reopening schools.

In one totally devastated town, on almost the only wall still standing, appeared one of those sayings of Mussolini: "La Voce Dei Cannoni Ecco L'Argomento Travolgente." This translates roughly as: "The voice of the cannons, here is the overriding argument." My companion contemplated the words, surveyed the surrounding desolation, and remarked, "How right he was! Eh, Bowman?"

Back at the Villa Piva, we learned that Bologna had fallen that day, which was also the Macmillans' twenty-fifth wedding anniversary. We celebrated both events that evening at dinner in my mess, with ice cream for dessert—the first ever served there. Mr. Macmillan asked me not to proceed to Bologna next morning, as I had intended, but to wait and go with him the following day, April 23. Mine not to question why. He was my boss. I agreed.

After a staff meeting on April 22, I was driven up the Via Emilia to Forli for the night, to ensure an early start the following day. Arriving at the Eighth Army command post at nine the following morning, I found the future Supermac ready to go and wanting to do it by jeep. This meant that at least one of us would have to ride in the back seat, and he insisted that we both do so. And so we proceeded northeasterly to Bologna—knees under our chins—the minister in tweed hunting coat, and the American colonel in beat-up field uniform.

As we traveled, Mr. Macmillan told me of problems coming up in Venezia Giulia, and particularly in Trieste.

By this time, of course, Marshal Tito, the communist-oriented Yugoslav Partisan leader, had long since become effective master of his own country, and a valued ally against the Germans. Technically, he was under the command of Field Marshal Alexander as supreme allied commander in the Mediterranean, but he also had some vested interests of his own in the Istrian peninsula, that little pendant into the Adriatic from its north shore, and the so-called Slovene Carso, surrounding Trieste.

Lately, my companion pointed out, Tito had been almost too successful, and it looked as though we might be confronted with a fait accompli—Yugoslav occupation of a substantial area that was to have fallen within the province of Allied Military Government and was considered an essential part of the supply line to Austria, where the next battles might well be fought.

All of this was interesting, of course, but I wondered why Mr. Macmillan thought it would be of special concern to me, who would have nothing directly to do with it. Or so I thought.

Before noon we rolled into Bologna, where I saw my first operating traffic signals in Europe. We switched from the jeep to a staff car flaunting my companion's five stars, and drove to the Municipio, or City Hall, which was to be the place where, for the next ten weeks, I would conduct the business for which my officers and I had been preparing for more than nine months.

In this massive, undamaged medieval building, when we arrived, there lay in state the bodies of two local liberal (communist?) leaders who had been executed by a fascist Black Brigade firing squad against the Municipio wall just before Allied troops entered the city two days earlier. Their blood still spattered the wall, sharing it with bouquets of flowers and the photographs of a multitude of other Bolognese who had been slaughtered during the dark preceding months.

From the flagstaff outside one of the windows of the office I was to occupy for the next several months, flew a red and white flag. Upon inquiry, I learned that the first troops into the city had, in fact, been those of the British Eighth Army's Polish Corps that had been bravely but obscurely fighting its way up the center of the peninsula. In honor of the victory, and to remind the world of the part played in it by the Poles, a Polish soldier had improvised a Polish flag by ripping down an Italian one, tearing off the green, turning the red and white stripes sideways and placing the remodeled banner where I found it.

Since only British and American flags were permitted to be displayed on public buildings, I caused the flag to be taken down and sent it to my wife, as a souvenir. Finding it stored away after my return to California, I offered it to Gen. Wladyslaw Anders, the Polish Corps commander, who had by then become a permanent resident of England. He was thrilled by the story, gratefully accepted the flag, and gave it a place in the Polish Military Museum in London.

The city itself appeared to be not in bad shape compared to others we had entered after long bombardment. The outskirts were a shambles, but there was little destruction of buildings in what we would, these days, call the inner city. It was, on the whole, a drab place except for the famous two leaning towers that are its symbol around the world. The buildings were all relatively flat—two or three stories high, with the second and higher stories extending over the sidewalks, sustained by pillars in a sort of uniform colonnaded effect—good for comfort in shopping on a wet or very hot day, but otherwise not very inspiring. I was to learn later that their beauty was in the courtyards and gardens within and behind.

Overall, the impression was one of very heavy population pressure over a long period of time. Building interiors were soiled and grimy. The Municipio itself had been the home not only of several thousand refugees but of their cattle and horses. Like many other public buildings in the Romagna, it had, as a matter of fact, been designed to accommodate animals. In addition to staircases, its architecture was characterized by floor-to-floor ramps up which the dignitaries of the Middle Ages were accustomed to ride their steeds directly into the anterooms of their offices.

Manure disposal had obviously been a problem. Wherever there was an open space or park, the manure of the immured animals had been arranged in neat, geometrically square piles, now covered by swarms of battening flies. In all of these things lay worries and work ahead for Allied Military Government.

A first priority, of course, was the matter of a suitable place for me to live. In this connection, I almost got into trouble. I was offered a comfortable housing arrangement as the paying guest of a very attractive and hospitable young countess whose mother owned one of the most swank palaces in Bologna. Just in time, Intelligence informed me that she had only within days lost her job (through his death) as the mistress of Signor Starace, the secretary of the Fascist Party. As they delicately put it, she had been in recent "direct contact with fascist personalities." Direct indeed!

The place I ultimately selected, after only a day or two of surveying the possibilities, was a palace high on a hill on the outskirts of the city, which I was informed had been the home of a very successful manufacturer and seller of pharmaceutical drugs. His name was Gazzoni and so we named the villa. Its exterior was reasonably austere, probably closer to Palladian than any other architectural style, but the interior was the most extravagant example of eighteenth century rococo possible to imagine. There was a private chapel in a separate structure down a garden path. The building was modern in such matters as plumbing and cooking facilities, and I was quite comfortable there in company with several of the women of my American Red Cross Disaster Relief team, who could not be suitably housed elsewhere in the devastated city.

It was also a great place to give a party, and so it was here about a month after I had settled in that my team gathered in the great ballroom to celebrate the first birthday of the activation of Emilia

Region. I cut a cake to the accompaniment of "Why Was He Born So Beautiful?" played by local musicians at the instigation of my senior assistants. There were some toasts and some photographs, and I think everybody had a great time. They were all wonderful people.

Partisans

Partisans passing in review before turning in weapons

It is hardly open to doubt that the greatest problem confronted by the United States in its military operations in Viet Nam was the activity of a communist-indoctrinated guerrilla force we called the Viet Cong. We recognized it to be the military arm of a partly indigenous, partly infiltrated, political force called the National Liberation Front. It was highly effective in hampering the conventional military operations of our forces and those of the Republic of (South) Viet Nam, which we then recognized as the legitimate government of the area where most of the fighting took place. The popular U.S. view was that there was something vaguely phony, if not outright dishonest, about its composition and operations.

Yet, at the time of which I am writing, the United States and its allies in northern Italy had adopted and put into effect exactly the same tactics, for similar motives, as we later attributed to our adversaries in Indochina. For many months we had been recruiting, arming, training, and infiltrating into northern Italy a guerrilla force whose mission of disruption and subversion is hardly distinguishable, except for time and place, from that of the Viet Cong. We directed the fighting potential of this force not only against the Germans but against the forces of the republican fascist government of the area, headed by the man who had headed the government of all Italy for two decades.

These guerrilla forces were the military arm of the National Committees of Liberation (even the name was the same as in Viet Nam) of northern Italy—comprised of non-fascist Italians to whom we had given assurances that, when the Germans were driven out, they would participate in the government of the areas where they operated and, eventually, in the government of a reunited Italy.

We called these forces the "partisans," which did not connote a particular party in all parts of northern Italy. There were partisans representing all the antifascist parties: Action, Christian Democrat, Liberal, Socialist, and Communist. All existed in substantial numbers in various areas of what we called the North, and we supported all of them. In Emilia Region, however, which had long been known as the Red Belt of Italy, the Garibaldi or communist category predominated virtually to the exclusion of the others.

In Emilia, it is fair to say, "partisan" was virtually synonymous with "communist," and we knew it. With rare exceptions, the only flags displayed, other than the Stars and Stripes and the Union Jack on AMG headquarters, were either the plain red banners bearing communist symbols or Italian flags similarly embellished. This circumstance had embarrassing aspects for our forces, and we took such cosmetic or ameliatory action as was feasible, including an effort—never quite successful—to substitute "patriots" for "partisans." This did not alter the fact that virtually all the people we dealt with in Emilia were in fact professed and unashamed Communists, who looked to Bologna, the Italian Kremlin, as their capital.

If anticommunism can be considered to be a valid foreign policy at all, it may be conceded that it has, by and large, constituted almost the entire foreign policy of the United States during most of the time since World War II. It is probably inevitable that under such circumstances a myth has at worst been created, or at best allowed to flower, richly fertilized by the press, that Northern Italy has recently "gone communist."

The idea that there has been a sharp turn left in my former military government domain during the last two decades is misconceived. The fact is that the communist officials who now administer the great ancient cities of Emilia, or the communist officials who preceded them, were installed by Great Britain and the United States as a matter of the highest national policy and enlightened self-interest during the last days of April and the early days of May 1945. One of the American political advisers who recommended this was Harlan Cleveland, more recently our ambassador to NATO. On the British side, Harold Caccia, late United Kingdom ambassador to the United States, concurred.

There is no occasion for shame or regret in this fact. Although the policy was presented at the time as a means of broadening the base of the Italian governmental structure, the basic power consideration was that the partisans who had helped win (some would say had won) the battle for northern Italy were not about to accept conservative heads of government in their provinces.

During the last week in April and the first week of May 1945, I appointed several communist prefects and mayors—sometimes against my own better judgment, but with faith in the system and backed by the probity and wisdom of my superiors. That it would have been foolhardy to do otherwise at the time is beside the point. We did it and should not hesitate to say so.

The classic case, of course, is that of Giuseppe Dozza, who was appointed mayor pro tem of Bologna, on instructions from the Allied Commission in Rome, within hours after Bologna fell. For almost a quarter-century thereafter, he conducted a clean, efficient administration, based on fiscal responsibility, a balanced budget, lower living costs, and ample incentives for the small businessman. He was a middle-class hero by every standard, and it is hard not to say, "If this be a Communist, let's have more of them in public office."

The problems created by our commitments to the partisans and the Committees of Liberation were my meat and drink for the next ten weeks. They came into particularly sharp focus in connection with two matters that had to be dealt with at once: first, the appointment of permanent prefects for the five newly liberated Po Valley provinces; second, the disarming of our own faithful guerrilla allies—some of whom, like all men who have become accustomed to living outside the normal rules, might have acquired a taste for it.

Under other conditions, even under the conditions envisioned when the commitments to the partisans and the Committees of Liberation had been made, these would not have been my problems. Had the Germans stood fast in the northwest toward Milan and Turin, the job would have been handled by men of higher rank, supported by thousands of troops.

As a matter of fact, the disarming of the partisans in Bologna province *was* accomplished by my superiors before they headed northwest to pursue the Germans and to keep France out of the Val d'Aosta. In the other four provinces, the job was mine, and the only tool for its accomplishment was simple persuasion.

The technique was well conceived and, on the whole, effective. Within the weeks following liberation, they were paraded, armed, with music and flags before a reviewing officer (in most cases, me) in each provincial capital and sizeable town. At the end of the parade route were placed several empty army trucks and some local spielers who continuously plugged the example of Garibaldi in discarding his weapon and returning to the plow when his work as a soldier was done.

Carefully coached bellwethers in the vanguard tossed their weapons into the trucks, and the rest followed suit, it having been previously announced that there would be certain refreshments and kudos for unarmed partisan veterans. Then the partisans again assembled, weaponless, in the plazas where their leaders and selected heroes received certificates, personally signed by Field Marshal Alexander, attesting to their valor and expressing British-American thanks for their efforts. In retrospect, it seems unbelievable that the scheme could have worked, yet it did.

There is ground for speculation that there was more to this miracle than met the eye—that certificates of valor, free lunches, and other kudos were only part of the reason for ready collaboration with our forces. Many historians now believe that the word may have come down directly from Moscow that Stalin had other important fish to fry at the moment and did not want to become embroiled controversially in Italian affairs at that time.

Nevertheless, despite careful planning, good luck and possible assistance from the Kremlin, there were some tense moments. One of the scariest of these occurred at the Parma disarmament ceremony on May 9. On this occasion, either the arrangements had not been handled with as much care as elsewhere or the partisan leaders were more hardheaded. The pre-throwaway parade went off normally, and I proceeded to another grandstand in front of the Municipio to await the arrivals of the presumably disarmed paraders. When they came in view, they were no less armed than when they had passed in review with their weapons.

There was nothing to do but proceed as if this had been expected. I made my speech and presented certificates to the leaders. At the same time I noted with uneasiness that someone had set up a free vino dispensary in one corner of the plaza. During the speech of the communist prefect that followed mine, one of the boys at the refreshment stand (having presumably had one too many) fired his weapon into the sky. As if on signal (and to this day I do not know that it was not), all six thousand guerrillas in the square, packed shoulder to shoulder as they were, fired their arms—machine guns, bren guns, rifles, and tommy guns—toward the sky.

The firing continued for about a minute, during which I stood there, the most prominent feature of the scene, thinking, "What if just one of those guys doesn't like colonels? or Americans?" But the moment passed; to my knowledge no one was even hurt, and the weapons were turned in within an hour.

Five prefects had to be appointed—each in his own capital with appropriate ceremony. About ten partisan standdown ceremonies had to be held, after ample and painstaking preparation, as my experience in Parma could attest. But this was by no means the total extent of the job to be done.

Fortunately, the task that came first, and was most urgent in every other part of Italy, was of minor importance here. There was no starvation, and the area was traditionally the most blessed of all Italy in natural food resources.

But all the other problems were present. The great universities had to be reopened, including the one at Bologna, oldest in Europe. So had the schools, and the banks, and the business and industrial enterprises of all kinds that had been closed during the siege. There were plenty of public health problems, and all the rest of the conglomerate that comprises the business of living and was the concern of military government. In tackling these problems I had, happily, the assistance of the best people in the business, and it went smoothly.

Whenever, during this period, I appeared officially in a town or at a university for any public purpose, I was likely to be offered some sort of honorary tribute—an honorary degree in the latter case, or a certificate of honorary citizenship in the former. This raised some ethical questions, particularly because of recent experience with a senior officer who had developed the process of collecting such memorabilia to the level of a fine art.

It has to be remembered that during that long winter five of the provinces of my region had been technically under the control of the American Fifth Army, whose senior civil affairs officer was a regular army medical officer, of a distinguished early American family. One of his top assistants was an Italian-speaking Navy Reserve commander, in civilian life a municipal judge in an eastern city and later a member of the supreme court of his state. Very often, during the winter, while the general and his staff occupied the Palazzo Vecchio in Florence, word came to me from my people strung along the line of the Apennines that they had hardly settled into many towns when an officer in naval uniform appeared, made his way to the *sindaco* (mayor), and addressed him in Italian along somewhat the following lines: "Signor Sindaco, the military governor has been informed of your desire to offer him honorary citizenship in your beautiful town [village, province] and is happy to accept. He will come here for the ceremony you have proposed on [date]. Now, I suggest that you erect the platform for the presentation on the east side of the piazza, and I think it would be well to have a band of not less than . . . pieces, etc."

In almost no case had the poor mayor or prefect ever heard of the general, much less thought of offering him anything, but of course, as other politicians in other places have been known to do, he played the game, then told me about it. It was a harmless enough caper, though to my mind somewhat degrading to the American image, and I admit I resented it, although I never did anything affirmatively to stop it. The Fifth Army commander was also a collector of honors, although to a much lesser degree, and it would not have been wise or operationally helpful to make an issue of the matter.

The net effect of this experience, however, was to make me very chary of accepting such kudos for myself, and I did so very sparingly, turning down honorary degrees as such completely, and accepting the honorary citizenship awards only when I was satisfied that the offer was entirely spontaneous and voluntary and that the donor's feelings would be hurt if I declined. In the case of Bologna, the offer of citizenship came several months after I had moved to Trieste, and I had no hesitation in visiting the old home town and accepting the certificate, which I can now see from where I hunt and peck. Mayor Dozza, who presented it, continued to hold that office for 25 years after that date.

Nor could I, without offending my academic hosts, decline to accept token testimonial medals offered on occasions of the openings of the universities of Ferrara and Bologna. The latter, following unduly complimentary reference to the donee as "distinguished soldier and military governor, protector and administrator" of Bologna and its university, testifies to the city's "memory of how the American and British armed forces, assisted somewhat by the local population, restored the pride and courage of the Italian people in defense of freedom, on 22 April 1945." Gratifying, and I hope at least partially true.

On April 28, Mussolini had been captured and killed, and his body was strung up by its heels in a Milan square in company with that of his mistress Clara Petacci. Ten days later the war in Europe came to a close and was celebrated in our mess by speeches and toasts in which possibly more nice things were said by Britons about Americans, and vice versa, than on any previous or subsequent occasion in history.

At about this time, one of my senior assistants uncovered and turned over to me a 1941 Buick, which was so totally American and so dashingly recent in design that it couldn't have been more ideal for my use. Not long afterward, the British Eighth Army News published a cartoon in which two soldiers commented bitterly on the "chrome-plated brew can" hanging from the back end of a low slung, civilian-type car. Since my Buick was the only car around that in any way resembled the one depicted, I am circumstantially convinced that the cartoon immortalized the American late model product that was to be a badge of office for me for the next two years.

For the benefit of the lay reader (or anyone who did not serve in the military either in North Africa or in eastern Italy during World War II), it should be explained that the brew can, for brewing tea on the road over either a wood fire or an alcohol stove, was standard equipment on every British registered vehicle in the Eighth Army area. Tea, heavily loaded with condensed milk, was served mid-morning and mid-afternoon without fail, from every such vehicle on the road. These pauses for refreshment at the roadside were a very comforting sight to fellow travelers, even those who did not share the tea tradition.

During the month that all this was going on, and in the light of the growing prospect that I might soon depart Bologna to become one of the characters in the drama at the head of the Adriatic, I still had some goals to achieve in Emilia-Romagna.

To view the events I have discussed in proper historical perspective, it must be remembered that much less than a century earlier each of the eight provinces in my charge had been an independent kingdom, dukedom, or the like. Whatever coordination had occurred between them for the common interest had been economic or social, not governmental. I was determined, if I could, to strike a blow before I left for some official arrangements that would promote regional unity of purpose and action in the future.

To this end, I convoked in early June what was probably the first meeting ever held of the heads of government of the erstwhile kingdoms and dukedoms. All eight prefects whom I had appointed attended, and all seemed to be a little surprised to learn what nice, agreeable people their counterparts from all those places up and down the Via Emilia really were. Dividends in terms of trade, business, public safety, and similar functions were realized within the few weeks I remained in Bologna after the meeting, and I was informed that the spirit of cooperation I tried to engender did in fact gratifyingly persist after my departure.

We also discussed at the meeting another matter that gave me some concern. While the program of disarming the partisans had worked remarkably well and every participant had turned in at least one weapon, there were rumors that some of the better and more efficient firearms were still out there in the hills in the hands of men long experienced in using them. One of the prefects who attended my meeting had himself been a dedicated and effective partisan, but there were other leaders who were not wholly satisfied and might be easy to involve in a threat to the peace under Allied Military Government.

One of the bits of evidence I submitted to the prefects to indicate that there were still people who might like to upset the government of which they were now a part, and replace it with a "pure" partisan regime, consisted of two sheets of postage stamps, printed by partisans, I was informed, after the disarming. In the end, the prefects agreed that some action should be taken to clarify the situation, to make it clear that there was only one official government in Emilia-Romagna—the Allied Military Government. Having foreseen the acquiescence of my prefects, I had had the necessary order prepared in advance, and it was published the following day.

Whether for this or some other reason, no one thereafter questioned our authority in any active or outward way, and Emilia-Romagna was turned over to the jurisdiction of the Italian government within a shorter period of time after liberation than any other region of Italy. There can be no doubt, of course, that the fact that the war had ended also played a part in this early transition.

In the remote, off-stage distance, I was dimly aware that the New Zealanders had entered Trieste on May 1 and wondered what they had encountered. Three weeks later came an official suggestion that I give up my job in Bologna and take over the military government at the head of the Adriatic.

I have spoken of the partisans of the Po Valley and the problems they presented to AMG administration and operations in Emilia-Romagna. Around the end of the Adriatic in the Istrian peninsula and the Slovene Carso, another brand of partisan stood ready to demand his share in the victory—a brand considerably less likely to be appeased by commendatory certificates, trinkets, or wine. He was, collectively, the Slavna IV Armija Maršala Tita—Tito's Fourth Army.

The Fourth Army was a regular Yugoslav military force organized in the spring of 1945 for the special purpose of marching on Trieste. It was composed mostly of soldiers who had been tempered in the crucible of fighting under the most primitive conditions. Each of them had, by his bravery, hardihood, and loyalty, fully earned the right to be where he was in his nation's forces.

At the time of which I write, many of these soldiers were in

Trieste and its environs. Since most of them were Slavs, they were a significant presence in an area that for a hundred years had been called Italia Irredenta—Italy unredeemed—by its Italian inhabitants. The translations for slave and Slav, in the English connotations of the words, are identical in Italian: singular, *schiavo*; plural *schiavi*. The latter in particular, pronounced skee-ah-vee, is a word that can easily be made to sound like a sneer. The initial "s" can be hissed for a second or two before the "kee-ah-vee" is released. It is a word that by its very sound often conveys sentiments of contempt, scorn, and disdain comparable to those expressed by "nigger" snorted by an unreconstructed southern redneck. Later I was to learn, in Trieste, that this was often exactly the effect and implication intended.

Some of the reasons for this hostility are rooted deep in the culture and history of the area. For centuries, the waterborne expatriates of the several Italian nations—Venice in particular—sailors and fishermen, had settled on the shores of the Adriatic almost as far east as Greece. There, as the years passed, they built great cities where there had been none or transformed the villages they found. From Rome and Venice and Florence, they brought an appreciation of art and music. They were sophisticated, cultured, and temperamentally mercurial.

The Slovenes and Croats (*Schiavi*) seemed slow, dull, and humorless to the mercurial men from the south. At best, they were clodhoppers—country bumpkins. As time passed, some of them came into the big city of Trieste to work in the shipyards or as domestic servants. A few, but not many, succeeded financially. When they did, they tended to join the majority, to speak the language of the city, and to take Italian names. Their infiltration, though not their integration into the Italian community, was encouraged by the Austrians who had ruled Trieste for four centuries before the Treaty of Rapallo in 1920 gave it to Italy. They felt the Slovene and Croat presence would tend to downgrade possible future Italian boundary claims. *Divide et impera*. Divide and rule. A very sound precept for conglomerate empires, and one that kept Austria-Hungary alive and viable beyond its time.

Despite the imputation of *schiavi* as hissed by the more racist Italians, Slavs were not fools or cowards, nor were they lacking in pride or intelligence. As a practical matter, however, until World

War II there was really very little they could do about the oppression and outrage to which they were subjected. When the Germans moved in, things became even worse, but the war provided opportunity for the first time for effective resistance. In Venezia Giulia, as elsewhere in Europe, the partisans became active, but with special motivation. During the second half of 1941, two years before the Italian capitulation, the Slovene National Liberation Front had begun organized and highly effective resistance to both the Italians and Germans. For their boldness, entire Slovene villages were destroyed and the inhabitants sent to German factories and farms.

By the end of 1942, the operations of Slovene partisans, both in Venezia Giulia and elsewhere, were conducted under the direction of the Yugoslav Army of National Liberation, which was the direct-action arm of Marshal Tito's Yugoslav National Liberation Committee. Eventually, they were joined by many of the Italian Garibaldini (communist) partisans who allowed ideology to outweigh nationality. By and large, however, the partisans of this area were Slovenes and, for practical purposes, a part of the Yugoslav army, which was otherwise composed of brother Slavs from further east who had now reached Trieste at the end of a long, rough war. When the Second New Zealand Division of 13th Corps met them there on May 1, 1945, they were not about to be dislodged.

The hinterland that the Slavs tilled and tended was pretty poor stuff, only about 14 percent arable. From its bleak littoral strip soon to the north rose the Giulian Alps—scenic, but not so much so as to provide tourist attractions that could compete with the nearby Dolomites, the Tyrol, or Switzerland. There were no known mineral resources of any consequence. Indeed, the area would have little geographic significance were it not for the central geographic fact that it includes the port of Trieste.

This fact had been responsible for the historical circumstance that the nearest European power, Austria-Hungary, maintained close surveillance of the area, and dominance over it, from the fourteenth century until 1918. During those centuries, it was a funnel through which poured supplies for northern Italy as well as every part of the Austro-Hungarian empire, which included practically all of central Europe. The people of the area, however, were not Austrian by either race, language, or custom. In the cities and particularly in Trieste, the great majority were Italians—merchants, traders, ship builders, industrialists. Educated and urbane, they enjoyed their own newspapers, schools, and cultural clubs. Even the irredentists, clamoring for reunion with Mother Italy, were tolerated under the benign rule of the empire.

This benign Austrian policy, rooted in a general evolution toward a more democratic form of government and the accelerated rate of industrialization that characterized the four decades preceding World War I, also benefited the Slovenes in Trieste. The need for additional industrial workers caused a population boom. Between 1846 and 1910, the population rose from 80,000 to 229,000. This influx came not only from the newly established Kingdom of Italy, but from nearby Austrian provinces as well. They were predominantly Italians, Slovenes, and Croats.

According to the 1910 census, Trieste was still an ethnically mixed city, with 148,000 Italians and 56,000 Slovenes constituting the major ethnic categories. The increase in the Slovene population had by 1914 understandably strengthened the Slovenes' economic, cultural, and political status. They were able to invest their savings in Slovene-controlled industries, banks, and cooperative savings institutions. They could read Slovene-language newspapers—specifically the liberal daily *Edinost* (Unity), founded in 1876—and pay dues to Slovene cultural clubs centered in a Slovene National Home (*Narodni Dom*) in the heart of the city.

In the Great War of 1914–1918, Austria-Hungary and Italy were enemies. The tolerant attitude of the state toward irredentism and the professed Italians of the area came to a shuddering halt. Many of them were interned, prosecuted, and persecuted. Mobs looted Italian ships in the harbor, hacked and wrecked Italian coffee houses, and burned to the ground the offices of the Italian–language newspaper *Il Piccolo*.

The First World War ended for this part of the world with the 1920 Treaty of Rapallo, by which Venezia Giulia, except for Fiume, was ceded to Italy. In 1924, by treaty following the overthrow by fascists of its free city government, Fiume also became Italian. Throughout the area, fascism and intolerant, virulent, fanatical Italian nationalism—greatly aggravated by memories of the humiliations of the war—became rampant.

Case records abound. On March 12, 1924, the wife of G. H., a Slovene clerk, gave birth to a child. The father applied for a birth certificate for his son, whom he had decided to name Gorazd. The Italian registrar refused to enter the name, and substituted the Italianized version Gerardo. The father protested in court. Rebuffed, he applied to a higher court, which held:

> The fact is that the obstinacy with which G.M. insisted in bestowing a Slavic name upon his son in this historic moment when everybody ought to take pride in Italianizing everything . . . arouses justifiable suspicion that a more or less concealed purpose lurks behind it . . . The right of paternity may not reach so far as to constitute an abuse to disturb the public order, or to offend the national consciousness . . . Appeal dismissed. (Copied from Allied Information Service press background information release)

In like spirit, and with like rationalization, Slovene language schools had been closed in the 1920s, and the children offered fascist prizes to learn Italian. The premises of Slovene newspapers were repeatedly invaded and despoiled by fascist youth, and the papers themselves were finally put out of business by Royal Decree in 1928. Villages in almost totally Slovene areas in the countryside were arbitrarily renamed in Italian. Slav cooperatives were destroyed; Slav priests, intimidated. Oppression had come, and with it, violence.

The Slovene National Home in Trieste was the principal Slovene cultural center of Venezia Giulia. It housed a theater, a hotel, a restaurant, a library, a music school, and many cultural societies. On the same day, this Slavic institution and its counterpart in Pola were burned to ashes. No one contended that this was a mere fortuitous coincidence.

The encounter between the New Zealanders and Marshal Tito's Fourth Army at Trieste had not been programmed as an adversary confrontation. The Yugoslav Fourth Army, and the British 13th Corps, of which the New Zealanders were a part, were both elements in a military force theoretically under the command of the supreme allied commander, British Field Marshal Harold Alexander. The war in Europe had not ended. Germany and Austria were the next targets. Trieste was considered the principal point of entry for supplies that would be needed in Austria, and both the

Yugoslav Fourth Army and the various elements of the British-American forces in Italy were expected to turn north after they met and to march side by side through or across the Alps to the next objective.

When the racially Slavic Fourth Army actually arrived in Trieste, however, it had become fairly evident that there would be no war in Austria. And by the time the New Zealanders met them there the war was substantially at an end. The Germans capitulated six days later. This permitted, in fact required, the devotion to political concerns of much time and energy that would otherwise have been devoted to fighting. The fact began to emerge that Tito and his troops had ideas about Trieste and its environs that far transcended its function as a way station on the road to Austria.

Yugoslav territorial claims to Venezia Giulia, and even to territory considerably to the west of it, had been asserted from time to time both before and during the war. In 1943, the Slovene Regional Council had "incorporated" into Slovenia the entire Slovene littoral, including Gorizia and Trieste, and the Croats of Istria took similar action as to that peninsula, including Pola. These actions were ratified in due course by the Yugoslav National Council, and Marshal Tito had approved them even while acquiescing in the general British-American position that no official Yugoslav claims should be made until the peace conference.

Well aware of all aspects of the problem, Field Marshal Alexander began discussions with Marshal Tito concerning it in the winter of 1944–45; and visited him in February 1945. Alexander considered it settled that when the British and American forces under his command joined the Yugoslavs in or near Trieste, the military government in the area would be turned over in due course to the same Allied Military Government that had by now accomplished the reconstruction of most of the rest of Italy.

However, by May 1, the world picture had changed radically. It was apparent to all that the war was just about over; Trieste might still be handy as a logistical base for the occupation of Austria, but the critical need envisioned earlier was rapidly fading away. The temptation presented to the Slav leader was great, and understandable. Applying the bird-in-the-hand principle, Tito and his troops moved into the city on May 1. Since his Partisans already had effective control of the environs and countryside, some of them were able, on the same day, to greet the New Zealanders at the Isonzo, thirty miles to the west. When the New Zealanders entered Trieste on the following day, it was firmly under Yugoslav control, although there were still some German troops cowering in public buildings, determined to resist the Partisans at least long enough to permit surrender to the Allied forces.

There ensued the period that the Triestini were later to refer to as "the forty days." The New Zealanders took the surrender of the German garrison following a short siege and moved into the port area, which it was essential to protect for future use in receiving supplies for points north. Meanwhile, the Yugoslavs occupied, and displayed their flag over, all important public buildings and issued proclamations assuming full control of governmental functions, commerce, and industry. As a portent of claims to come, it was ordered that on May 4 all watches be set back one hour "to conform to the time in the rest of Yugoslavia."

When the Yugoslav forces entered the city, the Italian Councils of National Liberation, composed of people who had worked underground against the Germans, greeted them as liberators but were forthwith disbanded and some members arrested. At a meeting called at short notice, hastily assembled candidates for a communist-type government were elected by acclamation. All demonstrations of pro-Italian sentiment were suppressed, often with gunfire. Many hundreds of Italians disappeared, and while it may be assumed that some merely left as a matter of prudence, there is no doubt that many were deported to the interior of Yugoslavia. The belief that many of these were simply slaughtered and their bodies tossed into the *foiba* (pits or caves that abounded in the hinterland) burgeoned among the Triestini.

An Allied Army observer reported, "Trieste is virtually under a military dictatorship; a reign of tyranny is operating against the Italian community." A local Italian resident wrote, "The town is living under a painful incubus, under a cloak of lead, and only the presence of Allied troops, though inactive spectators, gave the people a feeling of trust and hope for the future."

Despite the increasingly evident conflict of objectives between the Yugoslavs and their late western allies, there were no actual hostilities, nor was the city divided into zones. Soldiers of all armies involved circulated freely about the city and environs. The

New Zealanders took over Miramare Castle and turned it into a recreation area. The soldiers of both sides greeted each other civilly, but not warmly. In the words of Sir Geoffrey Cox:

> We came up against a barrage of reserve which discouraged any individual mixing in Venezia Giulia. We and the Yugoslavs met on the football field or at other sporting events. We got drunk together at formal dinners. We saluted each other's officers. But when the matches were over, the dinner done, you realized that though you might know Yugoslavs better, you did not know any one individual Yugoslav better. There was fraternization, but no friendship . . . As a result it was only toward the end of the first month of Yugoslav administration that any real contact developed at all, and then mostly in the villages and outlying areas. In Trieste itself, there was never any really close association comparable to that which grew up between the Italians and the British, American and New Zealand troops. (*The Race for Trieste*, p. 243)

The favored spellings of the words Yugoslav and Yugoslavia in those days were "Jugoslav" and "Jugoslavia." It was inevitable, considering the nature of the British, New Zealand, and American soldiers, that their late allies should become known as "the Jugs." There was nothing disrespectful or derogatory about this. Other military people on the peninsula had, of course, long before accepted designation as Yanks, Brits, Limeys, Eyeties, Kiwis, Aussies, and so on.

Confrontation of Allies

Reviewing stand at a partisan disarmament ceremony

Meanwhile, at the Kremlin, the White House, and No. 10 Downing Streeet, the subject was not being neglected. Even before the German surrender, British Prime Minister Winston Churchill had discussed the question of Trieste with President Harry Truman, suggesting the importance of the British and American troops arriving first, and recalling the importance the late President Roosevelt had attributed to Trieste as an international port serving the entire Danube basin. Mr. Truman had agreed, and on May 1 Field Marshal Alexander told the prime minister that he expected troops of the British Eighth Army to reach Trieste within 24 hours.

It was not soon enough for the purposes that had been suggested by Churchill to Truman. Instead of reporting his occupation of Trieste, as had been hoped, Alexander told Churchill that Tito's forces had entered the city on April 30, having occupied most of Istria beforehand. He also suggested to the prime minister that his own troops had a profound admiration for Tito's soldiers and would not accept happily orders "to turn away from the common enemy to fight an ally." On May 2, nevertheless, New Zealand troops under Gen. Bernard Freyberg entered Trieste, took the surrender of the German garrison, and occupied the dock areas two days before the general surrender of German forces in Italy.

Three days later, the field marshal suggested that Tito would doubtless be more amenable to easy transition of his troops in Trieste and Istria to British-American command if he were assured that when the city was no longer needed as a base for the war still to be fought in Austria, he would be allowed to incorporate it into his New Yugoslavia. In what was as close to a rebuke as the field marshal ever received from his prime minister, Churchill told him in effect to "lay off that line" and leave all such questions for the peace conference to come.

A week later, on May 12, the prime minister received from President Truman a message confirming substantial agreement with Mr. Churchill's views, stressing the harm that might be done in other contested places if a firm stand were not made here. Churchill reported this to the supreme allied commander and was consequently the more taken aback two days later by a further message from Mr. Truman urging a cautious approach through diplomatic channels and particularly deprecating any action that might tie up in Europe troops needed for the war still to be fought and won in the Pacific.

In the end, by whatever means, an accommodation was reached, with the concurrence of the major governments, which provided for the division of Venezia Giulia into two zones. The one to the west was to be occupied by British and American forces; the one on the east, by the Yugoslavs. These were called Zones A and B, respectively. Trieste was by far the most important city in either zone and contained about five-sevenths of the population of Zone A. Both zones were to be considered occupied and held in trust pending a peace conference. The line of demarcation between them was informally designated the Morgan Line, in recognition of the active and effective part played in the negotiations by Lt. Gen. Sir William D. Morgan, Field Marshal Alexander's chief of staff.

The Morgan Line is sometimes said to have been arrived at on the basis of geographical factors making it militarily defensible, but my associates who knew more about such things than I did, laughed at the idea. It did indeed generally run parallel to and east of a secondary road to Tarvisio and the Austrian border, which Alexander contended he must have as part of his supply route for Austria, but was never in fact used for this purpose.

According to the story of its origins that I consider most credible, it was simply doodled on a map by staff officer Arch Hamblen, as he sat respectfully following the negotiations being carried on between Alexander and Tito. As he listened, he drew a line that included the city of Trieste, some of its environs, and a narrow strip to the east of the Isonzo Valley Road. Feeling that much more talk would have to precede the adoption of such an important boundary, Hamblen was amazed when the higher-ranking negotiators glanced at his doodle and, after the manner of soldiers accustomed to making quick decisions, adopted it.

It was along and across this line that most of the trouble during the ensuing two years would occur. Made part of the Iron Curtain by Winston Churchill in his Westminster College speech, it became a geographical symbol of the division between the East and the West—between democracy and totalitarian communism—the battle line of the Cold War Marne.

In any event, the line so adopted became official on the governmental level by written agreement (thereafter called the Belgrade Agreement) signed in the Yugoslav capital and further clarified by a supplemental agreement signed by Generals Morgan and Jovanović at Duino Castle in the British-American zone on June 20. A directive from Allied Force Headquarters dated June 26 clarified the structure and charter of the Allied Military Government, providing inter alia that:

    1. The administration should be integrated Anglo-American, following the pattern established in Italy.
    2. Nothing should be done that would in any manner prejudice the ultimate disposition of the territory by a peace conference.
    3. Except in serious emergency situations the Morgan Line should be open to free civilian passage and commercial traffic.
    4. Local government should be based generally on the Italian

pattern, using such elements of the existing Yugoslav civil administration as may be working satisfactorily, but applying the word "administration" (as used in the Belgrade Agreement) to mean personnel, not institutions.

5. The civil law in effect would be that of Italy on September 8, 1943, but there would be no right of appeal to Rome from the civil courts; all legislation of the fascist republic and the German and Yugoslav occupations was repealed.

6. The People's Courts, which the Yugoslavs had created to try fascists, Nazis, and collaborators would be abolished, but persons in these categories would be interned.

7. Metropolitan and AMG lire would be the only acceptable legal tender.

Later, the Combined Chiefs of Staff confirmed all of these interim instructions with only minor changes, and they became the permanent pre-peace treaty occupation charter of the military government I was called forward to administer west of the Morgan Line.

The Casa del Fascio, a fine modern building that had formerly housed the local fascist hierarchy (and as this is written is the metropolitan police headquarters of Trieste), had already been renamed Casa del Popolo and requisitioned as the headquarters for Allied Military Government, when I arrived there on the Fourth of July, 1945. Eight days earlier, the Charter of the United Nations had been formally signed in San Francisco. Twenty-two days later, the first atomic explosion would take place at Almagordo; Hiroshima and Nagasaki were to meet their atomic nemesis a month later, followed in short order by the Japanese surrender.

After inspecting my office, I was taken to the villa that had been requisitioned for me high on the hillside overlooking the harbor and almost everything else of consequence in Trieste. The next day, I went to work.

The Domain

General Harding inspecting troops, May 2, 1946

Over the thirty-odd years since I left my post at the head of the Adriatic, I have often been referred to, either by way of introduction before making a speech or as background for something I have written, as the person who conducted the military government of Trieste following World War II. This is not quite accurate. The person in charge of the administration of the city as such was always a senior assistant—for example, Henry P. Kucera, city attorney of Dallas, in the first instance. Trieste is a name with a certain notoriety, and it would have been easy for the newspaper reader at home at the time I was there to assume that the area under Allied control was the city alone.

Such was not the case. To the west, my responsibility extended almost to the eastern end of the Gulf of Venice, and to the north, in a sort of panhandle, to the Austrian border. This strip to the north included the important city of Gorizia with a substantial Slovene population. The name of this city has long been applied by historians and military tacticians to a route (Gorizia Gap) from the USSR through compliant Romania and/or Hungary, just south of the point where the Alps fade out to the east. Then, as now, it offered easy access to Western Europe for an aggressor from the northeast. Today this is a matter of no less concern than it was in the late forties, particularly in the event of a shift in Yugoslav national policy now that Marshal Tito is dead.

Another small but world-famous community located north and east of Trieste near the border between the zones was Lipizza (Lipica), home of the famous Lipizzaner studs (named for the town and retaining the name in other places) that were the progenitors of the horses of the world-famed Spanish Riding School in Vienna. Parenthetically, Capt. Richard Weeber, who had been one of my officers in Emilia Region, was instrumental (following Gen. George Patton's statement of resolve on the subject) in the rescue and return to a new home in northern Austria of a number of the Lipizzaners that the Germans had been in the process of moving to a new location in northern Germany.

For the reader old enough to remember World War I, it will be of interest that the panhandle also included historic Caporetto, scene of a disastrous defeat for Italian arms in October 1917, in which more than 100,000 Italian soldiers were casualties. Many of the dead are buried in what may be the most dramatic military cemetery in the world, on a hillside near Redipuglia, also a panhandle community.

The best time to enjoy the vista of the port and city of Trieste is early evening, when the lights in the streets and buildings have been turned on, yet the colors and shapes are still evident. Under such conditions, which I enjoyed many times when returning to my city from business in the Isonzo Valley, or Monfalcone, or Rome, it bursts upon the eye with ineffable radiance as the traveler passes behind Miramare Castle and the prospect becomes unobstructed. It is fairyland, the stuff dreams are made of. It is possible at that moment to imagine that everyone living in such a place would be so happy just to be there that he would be filled with love for his neighbor and all about him.

The castle itself is worth a look, although tastes in castles differ. Not everyone is similarly touched by the place that was the home of Austrian Grand Duke Ferdinand Maximilian von Hapsburg (better known as Maximilian) before he took off with his beloved Carlotta about the time of our Civil War to become Emperor of Mexico on invitation from Napoleon III. As we all know, he met his death there when Napoleon withdrew his troops. This gave the castle a bad luck image that was not enhanced by the fates of most of its later occupants, including Franz Ferdinand D'Este, whose assassination at Sarajevo triggered World War I.

The interior of the castle was "improved" by some of its more recent tenants to a point where much of its charm has been obscured or dissipated. However, its stark white marble exterior, situated on a rocky point jutting into the sea just before Trieste comes into distant view, is the prototypical structure of fairy tales and days when knights were bold. During my time, it was the headquarters and quarters for the commanders of several successive British divisions, and eventually of Trieste United States Troops (TRUST).

The traveler exploring the city itself must be entranced by its riva, or waterfront, usually with a few ships standing by, its many piazzas, narrow winding streets, Roman theater, and beautiful buildings of varied architectural styles—all dominated by the great hill of San Giusto with its castle, churches, and park where the *alabardo* (the halberd of the city's heraldic shield) fell long ago when St. Sergius was martyred in Persia.

Imposing and monolithic, the Castle of San Giusto sits atop a hill of the same name in the center of the town. Despite its menacing aspect and warlike architecture, however, it has but very little history, and that neither warlike nor romantic. The Venetians built it in 1369 and dedicated it to St. Mark. It was intended as protective armament for the city, aimed primarily at the Turks. When the Venetians left, it was demolished; but before many years it was rebuilt by the Austrian protectors, who found its strong walls comforting while they watched from their hilltop for signs of invasion or sedition.

There have been more recent plans to demolish the castle, but this has never happened. It was used from time to time as a barracks or military depot and, finally, as a sort of museum for armor, arms, medieval furniture, and paintings. The courtyard was transformed into a stage or auditorium for musical programs or variety shows, including, with its increasing popularity as a new art form, grand opera. Its pit section alone can accommodate 3,500 numbered seats, and the view from the walls by either day or night is spectacular. The former royal box was one of the pleasanter perquisites of my temporary suzerainty.

Trieste boasts another theater, by the way, where grand opera and other live entertainment are presented in the colder months, which of course outnumber ones when evenings outdoors are bearable. It is an impressive house named after the great Italian operatic composer, Giuseppe Verdi. Inevitably, it soon came to be known to us irreverent Americans as Joe Green's.

The city also has more than its share of historical monuments honoring a multitude of persons and events, ranging from Emperor Charles VI of Austria to the dead of both world wars.

The churches of Trieste are varied and numerous. Triestini consider the Serbo-Orthodox church near the sea one of the most beautiful, with its round gold domes and countless spires. The Greek Orthodox church is another impressive structure, exhibiting tall Ionic columns of gleaming white stone. For a picture of village life centering about a small church, Opicina, with its trim paths and ageless history, is a fine example. The church of Opicina lies in the center of the village and rises high above the buildings.

Museums and art galleries record impressively the history of culture in Trieste, as well as the more modern art of the city. The civic museum at Piazza Venezia, Museo Civico Revoltella, was opened in 1812 and offers a remarkable collection of valuable paintings. The palace in which the museum is housed was left to the city in 1869 by Barone Pasquale Revoltella. The Orso Lapidario is an outdoor museum founded in 1843 at the spot where the old cemetery of San Giusto once was. Here there are displayed vestiges of Roman and medieval architecture. Two altars that were built by Roman soldiers still remain, as do numerous gravestones and other historic items. Near the Orso Lapidario is the Museo Civico di Storia ed Arte. Its collection contains a large assortment of ancient sculptures, vases, paintings, and fragments of various old utensils.

Along with the museums, art galleries play an important part in the city's cultural life. The Galleria d'Arte exhibits modern art. The Galleria d'Arte al Corso, which shows historical and modern furnishings and paintings, the Galleria Alto Scorpione on Via Rossini, and Galleria Alta Strega, are also among the city's many places of artistic exhibition.

I must not let myself be so carried away by my memories of the physical beauty of Trieste that I forget to point out that, to a much greater extent than Florence, Rome, Naples, Venice, and other Mediterranean cities to which it might be compared in the matter of aesthetic amenities and structures, Trieste was, and is, also pre-eminently a city of banking, insurance, commerce, and industry. The Assicurazioni Generali, headquartered in the city, had been the largest insurance company in Europe before the war. The Lloyd Triestino and other steamship lines straddled the world with their far-reaching routes. Several great shipyards built ships of all sizes and shapes, harboring possibly the world's greatest reservoir of shipbuilding skills. The port itself, divided into several sections, and the rail net that served it as well as the rest of the city, were as impressive.

All of these industrial and commercial enterprises contribute to the dramatic aspect of the city not only with their derricks, scaffolds, piers, rails, and bridges, near the port, but also through the office buildings, sometimes in other parts of the city, where company executives make their decisions and the administrative work is done.

To me, Trieste is an ideal city to wander in, carefree, pausing occasionally for a capuccino or to observe some incident characteristic of the life of the place.

During my time, the most characteristic incident likely to be observed was the demonstration. With its color, sound, displays of flags and posters, and the vented emotions of large aggregations of noisy people, it was easily the institution for which Trieste was best known around the world. No event or cause was too mean or inconsequential to provide the necessary occasion and incentive: the arrival of a distinguished or influential visitor who someone fancied might be able to exert some influence on the city's future; a holiday or holy day with ethnic or cultural overtones favorable or unfavorable to one of the factions; a bicycle race originating in metropolitan Italy. You name it. No further excuse was needed.

There were two principal kinds of demonstration: planned and spontaneous. Spontaneous was obviously the most appealing, and each element of the population striving for recognition, preeminence, and dominance usually claimed that its demonstrations were of that kind, although the spontaneity was in many cases highly suspect. There comes to mind the spectacle of several hundred middle-aged and elderly women, all in black from head to toe, as if in uniform, who would from time to time present themselves before the building that housed the seat of my government, at exactly four o'clock in the afternoon, to chant and cry about the starvation to which their families were being subjected. At some time from a half hour to an hour later, these ladies would at precisely the same instant terminate their lamentations, pick up their baskets and shawls and be out of sight in an instant. It was time, I am sure, to start thinking about dinner.

Actually, as time went on, the pretense of the unplanned or spontaneous demonstration wore too thin for credibility. In the case of the pro-Yugoslav demonstration, it simply was too much to expect us to swallow that hundreds or even thousands of people from the hinterland, who in the normal course of their lives had not been in the city half-a-dozen times, should just happen to be there, moved by similar emotions, after a grueling, all-night march on foot from the outlying communities where they lived and worked. Nor could we be expected to believe that hundreds of Triestini of similar political views, similarly dressed and equipped, just happened to be in the vicinity of the place where an event deemed antithetic to their political views was about to take place. Obviously, there was organization and leadership on both sides, and gradually this came to be tacitly admitted. Finally, we were able to institute and enforce a rule that every demonstration required a permit, which during my time we granted freely.

To avoid the confrontations between opposing factions that provided the real danger of violence, the demonstrations were restricted geographically; that is, they were required to be held in a certain piazza or series of streets. Sometimes two demonstrations conducted by opposing factions had to be authorized for the same time. When this was necessary, the trick was for the participants on one side or the other *spontaneously* to break out of the area assigned to them and cross the line of march of the opposing faction, at which point the peaceful demonstration could erupt into a free-for-all.

Of the unauthorized demonstrations to which both sides upon occasion resorted after the permit system was put into effect, perhaps the most difficult to control were the real or purported funerals. These were troublesome indeed. Often the funeral was bona fide, the corpse really quite recently having been a live person. In other cases, there can be no doubt that the body was abstracted from an inventory of cadavers maintained for the purpose of justifying a demonstration not previously authorized, by presenting it as a burial procession. There were many documented instances in which the body had been buried long ago and had been exhumed, presumably for the purpose of reburial in a more suitable location, or one more acceptable to the survivors. And there was no doubt that the routes of these processions, in which the hand-carried casket was the central feature, were deliberately selected to penetrate into enemy territory for the specific purpose of evoking an adversary reaction.

For the more massive and static demonstrations, sometimes in the guise of an athletic event, or the celebration of some obscure holiday sacred to one side or the other, the many piazzas of the city were ideal. The Piazza del Unita was the favorite. It was centrally located and easily policed. Flanked by the architecturally massive Palazzo del Governo and Municipio (seats respectively of area and city government), my colleagues and I could monitor the action from the balconies without getting personally involved; it was also my choice, although I am sure the participants could not have cared less about that.

The Piazza Garibaldi had a special feature that made it attractive to demonstration planners specifically seeking disorder. One of the narrow streets leading out of this popular focus for disruption started in the middle of one side of the open space and ascended, in a southerly direction, a hill that overlooked the piazza. This ascending thoroughfare, like many of the streets in Trieste and other parts of Europe, was paved with sharp-edged paving stones. A favorite tactic of the disrupters was to gain control of this upgrade, pry out one paving stone, and thereupon have available an almost limitless supply of lethal projectiles to rain down on the vulnerable enemy in the piazza below.

The city government of Trieste for some strange reason found it impossible to cope with this problem. The paving blocks were painstakingly replaced after each encounter, ready for use the next time. I was forced to solve the problem personally, which I did by ordering a thick layer of blacktop spread over the paving stones. It worked beautifully. Disorders in the Piazza Garibaldi continued, but they no longer featured the lethal hail of sharp-edged cubes of flinty stone.

There are those who, without denigrating the attractions of Trieste, assert with some heat that there is nothing unique about it, and this may be true. It certainly features elements of Venice, Naples, Vienna, and many other Italian and central European cities. In my time, it was better known than any city in the world for the demonstrations and disorders to which I have referred and will refer again, but this cannot be thought of as a permanent quality of uniqueness, particularly as today Yugoslav soldiers on holiday peacefully stroll its streets, sometimes even in the company of local girls. But Trieste does have one thing uniquely its own among cities: the Bora.

In southern California we have a similar but much milder phenomenon we call the Santana or Santa Ana—the former if you live in the city bearing the latter name. It is a wind that blows from the mountains toward the sea, contrary to the normal order of things; and in the city at the head of the Adriatic, it is called the Bora. You won't find that in a standard Italian dictionary. In essence, it is a wind roaring down through Alpine passes to the littoral. In intensity and the quality of making its presence felt and feared, there is nothing quite like it anywhere I have been, before or since the winters of 1945–46 and 1946–47.

The Bora is unique both in its direction and its extremely localized character. It is the master wind. In the summertime, known by other names but still blowing in substantially the same direction, it has many consequences. One of them is that people are blown into the water. Another, that during the heartiest blow the water itself being blown *from* the shore is likely to be no more than mildly choppy, and heavy seas are extremely unusual. Although this great wind, which is said to reach speeds of one hundred miles an hour upon occasion, blows in a serious way only a few days a year (and even on those days is not much more serious than the lake front breeze on Michigan Avenue in Chicago), the city is designed to a considerable extent around it. Home sites are selected with a view to protection from it, and the homes themselves are built with double windows behind high walls for gale protection. In some of the sidewalks there are holes wherein, during the Bora, stakes are set with chains strung between to keep pedestrians from blowing into the road, and the waterfront is similarly protected to prevent them from blowing into the sea. The Bora is important also in the tradition (or mythology) of the town, assuming in Trieste the place that Paul Bunyan held in the North Woods. The exploits of Paul's Big Blue Ox were not much greater than the playful antics of the Bora, which the Triestino will relate quite seriously. During the winter of 1946, a skeptical military statistician and researcher carried on an intensive investigation to find authentication of the story of the streetcar blown on its side or into the sea. He was unsuccessful, but the story goes on and so do others of the prowess of the Bora.

Having been required to deal with the problem of controlling mobs for many years of my life in the military, I have been heard to say with some conviction that a heavy rainstorm was the riot policeman's best friend; nothing else will break up a demonstration as effectively and quickly, regardless of the intensity of the feeling of the participants or the nature of the personal or ideological motives that may have been responsible for the demonstration in the first place. I misspoke and was careless both in thinking and memory. The Bora is a much more effective institution than the rainstorm for the purpose. Unfortunately, it is less likely to make its appearance in the summer months when the keeper of the peace needs it most.

I felt that the Bora was a sufficiently serious threat to the comfort and safety of the Triestini so at one time I instituted a system whereby its coming could be detected far from the city, and warning whistles could be sounded in the town to enable the people to prepare for it. For some reason, despite their respect for and concern about their famous native gale, the Triestini thought this warning system was the most hysterically ridiculous idea they had ever heard of, and it was the subject of many goodnatured jibes in the local press.

Summer 1945

Reactivating a Scout troop: "On my honor I will do my best . . ."

Although it might strain the credulity of the average American at home who reads scare stories about riots, demonstrations, and strikes in the Balkan powder keg, actually the summer of 1945 was relatively peaceful as I settled into my new role. Certainly there were public disorders, but we were learning to control them, and the violence was seldom lethal. Trieste had its share of bombings, fires, and shootings, but probably not in greater volume or intensity per capita than New York or London during the same period. I believe it to be a fact that during the entire last half of 1945 not a single life was lost as a direct consequence of public disorder. Virtually every murder or bombing, when thoroughly investigated, proved to be motivated by love, hate, greed, jealousy, or one of the other deadly sins, rather than by political considerations.

There were some special factors and forces to be coped with during those months. One of them was the world impact of the British general elections during the month of my arrival. As the world soon learned to its great amazement, the party of which the number one hero of the late war, Prime Minister Winston Churchill, was the leader, was defeated and replaced by a Labour government headed by an unimpressive and unpicturesque lawyer/teacher/social worker/politician named Clement Richard Attlee. This development was ecstatically hailed by the communists, not only in our administrative zone but in Yugoslavia and the USSR, as "the communist victory in England." The press and all pro-Yugoslav and pro-Russian political and propaganda bodies prophesied great changes in British foreign policy. They were soon set right. New Foreign Minister Ernest Bevin's tone at the next conference did not differ materially from that of his predecessor. Gradually it became clear that there would not be any important change, that England was still not completely the Soviet Union's brother in communism, and that England still intended to enforce by her own means what she conceived to be her interests in the Balkans. At first the Yugoslavs hoped that this was a merely temporary situation, a sort of lag between the expression of the will of the people and the catching up of events, but gradually the truth permeated and disillusionment set in. Anti-British propaganda became even more bitter and vitriolic than before the election.

Locally, the project calling for highest priority attention was the removal from the streets and waterfront of the physical signs of war: pillboxes, tank traps, barbed wire, and the like, left over from the fighting and particularly the Germans' last stand.

Half of Trieste's port facilities had been destroyed or seriously damaged. In Pola the damage was about 40 percent. In many places, breaks in the sewers discharged sewage into the streets. Bridges had been destroyed. The gas plant was damaged, and many of its mains had been ripped open by the bombing. Land mines were a continuing hazard.

In this matter the corps commander, Lt. Gen. Sir John Harding, interceded personally, as he rarely did, to influence my priorities. Sir John felt strongly that one way to help stem violence was to remove from sight the things that suggested it. A peaceful-looking city was more likely to be a peaceful city in fact. I could not but agree. My problem was that the channels through which approval for the expenditure of funds for any sort of public works, like similar channels in any other bureaucracy, did not respond at once to urgent demands.

The officer responsible for Public Works and Industry, excellent person though he was in all other respects, was deeply devoted to the bureaucratic methodology and channels for the job. I separated Public Works from Industry, recruited as its chief a professional contractor, an American who had virtually rebuilt Florence during the preceding year. I told him to get workers swarming over those pillboxes and tank traps, demolishing them with knives and forks if nothing more effective could be found. Much more effective means in fact were found, and the most urgent parts of the job were substantially completed by the end of the summer.

Another troublesome matter during these months was that of the so-called "deportees." Undeniably, during the forty days of Yugoslav occupation, a considerable number of Italians and non-communist Slovenes had disappeared from their normal surroundings and their homes. In many of these cases, there were witnesses to testify that they had been forcibly taken away by Yugoslav troops, partisans, or parties of civilian kidnappers who were presumed to represent the occupier. In other cases, they simply disappeared. This shortly became one of the sorest and most difficult problems with which I had to deal. The understandable position of their Italian relatives and friends in all cases was that, of course, they had been abducted against their wills. Since Allied policy had required us to tell these people that the Italian government could do nothing for them, and we had forbidden them to communicate with that government, naturally they presented their grievances to us.

They were sore grievances indeed, as the loss of loved ones must always be. On the other hand, our orders were clear: our bosses in Rome, Caserta, and Washington had warned us in the strongest terms that our mission was strictly confined to the interim administration of Allied-occupied Venezia Giulia; that we must not become involved with international matters or engage in any business that involved national governments. With regard to the matter of deportees our instructions were simple: to receive the complaints and forward them to higher authority for handling on the diplomatic level. These instructions we could not report to local civilians who throughout the first year continued to harass and worry us with this problem that so completely absorbed their interest.

In due course, a list was prepared containing, in the aggregate, about three thousand names of persons missing from their homes. A full investigation of each case was impossible, so after such action to assure bona fides as was possible locally, we merely compiled the information and sent it to Allied Force Headquarters, and thereafter continued from time to time to press for some action that we could report to our citizenry.

In the course of time, many of the alleged deportees returned. Some were, in fact, released by the Yugoslavs, but a considerably larger number merely came back on their own from places to which, for reasons that need not be queried or analyzed, they had thought it prudent to flee when entry of the first Yugoslav troops, and later British-American forces, was imminent. Our inability to act positively or to produce concrete results caused much disillusionment among the local people and cost us considerable loss of credit.

Intertwined with the deportee problem was the institution or tradition of the *foiba*—a word that does not appear in any of my small Italian dictionaries, and that I have never heard used in relation to any other place.

Many times and places have their own special tradition with regard to the means of inflicting death as a result of vigilante or mob law. The Salem witches were burned. In our pioneer west, the horse thief was hanged by setting him astride his horse with a noose suspended from a tree limb around his neck, then whacking the horse to drive it out from under him. The French Revolutionary mobs used the guillotine, the conspirators in medieval Italy and Sicily, the dagger and poisoning. Venezia Giulia also had a tradition: that of casting the victim/culprit into a pit (*foiba*) and sealing the entrance.

As time went on and some of the deportees failed to return, it was rumored that they had been made victims of this traditional institution and had been thrown either fully alive and whole, wounded, or dead into deep pits. Some of the holes were constructed for that purpose; others were the entrances to abandoned mines or caves in various parts of the limestone karst and Slovene littoral. *Foiba* was used generically to describe both the place and the act.

There is factual evidence in support of this, also. During the occupation, human remains were found in considerable numbers in mines, pits, caves, and quarries both within Zone A and elsewhere. In most cases, however, by the time the discoveries or exhumations were made, the bodies had suffered such an advanced degree of disintegration as to be completely unidentifiable, at least by locally available methods. In some instances, the victims were obviously soldiers, as indicated by bits of metal equipment or identification tags. In most of these cases, it appeared that the pits were merely convenient burial places; there were usually indications on the skull of heavy blows or the use of firearms. In almost every case, it seemed likely that death had occurred before May 1945. All of this does not prove a great deal one way or the other, since the *foibas* in which the missing Italians, if any, met their end, were undoubtedly in the more remote portions of the Yugoslav zone of occupation, or even in metropolitan Yugoslavia, and, hence, not accessible for examination.

What Triestine Italians understandably omitted to point out is that the *foiba* was not an institution invented by the Yugoslavs. In that locality, it was an ancient institution celebrated in song and stories for at least one hundred years before 1945 and almost certainly used against recalcitrant Slovenes and partisans during the fascist period and the early days of the war to an extent at least as great as its subsequent use by the Yugoslavs. The primitive art in the countryside, such as the sculpture in the line drawings of indigenous artists, indicates that this horrible means of inflicting death on one's enemies has been a favorite subject for many years, captivating the imagination and chilling the blood of the persecuted Slovene long before the Italian ever had cause to worry about its use against him.

The deportees I have described were people local to our zone who had been taken away and had to be found and brought back, if possible. The other side of the coin—constituting a different kind of problem no less onerous and pressing—was the matter of the refugees and displaced persons swarming *in*. It was a convention of nomenclature during the Italian operation that a "refugee" was an Italian displaced person, and a "displaced person" was a non-Italian refugee.

Many of the refugees were soldiers from Italian military units long since disbanded or from German prison camps. Others were Italian civilians fleeing in fright from the Yugoslav-occupied areas of Venezia Giulia. A large proportion of the displaced persons were Jews who had fled the Holocaust and slave laborers conscripted by the Nazis from many central European countries, now liberated, trudging homeward.

In the aggregate—refugees and displaced persons alike—they were homeless, uprooted by war, and cast adrift.

They had one common characteristic—hunger. They had to be housed, fed, and sped on their way. To provide the necessary food and shelter, we set up two refugee camps in Trieste, one in Pola, and one in Gorizia. Almost eighteen hundred were processed in July, over eleven thousand in August, almost five thousand in September. Most of the refugees and DPs spent only a few days in the camps before being dispatched either directly to their homes or to more permanent and commodious camps farther south.

The general situation, and particularly the housing shortage, were greatly aggravated by an influx of persons of all nationalities from all kinds of places, who required no help and were financially self-sufficient, but apparently just wanted to live in Trieste. In the early days of the occupation, it had been said that most of these were ethnic Yugoslavs sent in by Tito to change the ethnic character of the territory for purposes of a possible plebiscite or related motives. There were no doubt some such, but later observation and inquiry confirmed that these were greatly outnumbered by Italians, many of them voluntary refugees from the Yugoslav zone of occupation, who still regarded Istria as their home (as it had been for centuries in many cases) and wanted to stay as close to it as they could without actually being subjects of a government operated by their historic opponents.

The economic independence of these people was in many cases based on outside assistance, including bona fide public charity administered by the Italian Red Cross, Papal Relief, and similar agencies. We could not oppose this, although naturally we would have preferred, in view of our own shortages of housing, that the people be moved to Italy and the charity administered there.

Information received from Italian leaders in their more candid moments, added to my own observation and interrogation of some of the new Triestini of this class, caused me to conclude then (and I have had no occasion to change this opinion) that the assistance rendered to these people in the form of money, food, clothing, and other necessities of subsistence by private Italian citizens in Italy and public Italian agencies was given precisely for the purpose of keeping as many Italians as possible in Trieste.

It is hard to quarrel with this intention. I point out only that the Italian practice was precisely what they accused Tito of doing, and for the same motive—to increase the evidence of the Italianity of the territory, in preparation either for a plebiscite or for inspection by the representatives of the United Nations, the foreign ministers of the world, or anyone else who might play a role in the actual final disposition of the area. Official figures toward the end of my time in Trieste showed a population increase in the zone of about ten thousand, which is no small number when a lot of housing has been destroyed and the prewar population had been only three hundred fifty thousand. However, unofficial estimates submitted by my assistants who had to deal with the problem of sheltering these people suggest a total three or four times as great.

Nevertheless, somehow or other we coped. The situation was rife with opportunities for graft to obtain housing preference. I watched it closely and found little or none. This, in itself, was an achievement.

Interspersed with all the difficulties of coping during the summer were a few soft spots—times when we and our adversaries, or we and the local people, forgot the massive issues that divided us and met socially on the most gracious and amicable terms.

Such opportunities arose, for example, from the activities of the Joint Economic Committee, which had been set up under the Duino or Morgan-Jovanović Agreement as a device to ensure minimum interference with the normal economic life of Venezia Giulia as a whole, particularly as it required transactions, deliveries, enforcement of contracts, and the like, across the Morgan Line.

This committee was not in a strict sense a military government instrumentality, and its secretary was appointed by Allied Force Headquarters. However, since it dealt with what was essentially low-level civilian business, most of the members on both sides were military government officers, and as a practical matter it became the common conduit for routine business between the Yugoslav and British-American military governments. As time went on and the members grew to know each other as individuals rather than political adversaries, a degree of camaraderie developed. I entertained some of the Yugoslav members of the committee at my quarters (now renamed Villa California), and the head of our economic section was host to the committee as a whole, including the Yugoslav members, at a cocktail party at a local restaurant. (Throughout the occupation, restaurant food was considered black market and off limits.)

The Yugoslavs either wanted, or felt required, to reciprocate. Their first gesture was an invitation to visit the resort town of Abbazia (now Opatija), where their military government headquarters was located. As it happened, the date of the party was set for August 10. Our caravan lined up early, about ten cars strong. In those days, the project in hand was considered a bit adventurous. Although the term "Iron Curtain" had not yet been coined, the Morgan Line was even then regarded locally as something of the sort.

I was already in my car when I heard an unusual amount of whistle-blowing about the city, and upon inquiry was informed, to my satisfaction as an American but with some embarrassment in view of my plans for the day, that the Japanese had capitulated and, hence, all combat aspects of World War II were now history. Since the atom bomb and the USSR's declaration of war against Japan had virtually ensured the event, the news was hardly a surprise. I decided to go ahead with our plans, after sending word back to my office that the rest of the day and the following day would be holidays for all, and that a staff meeting scheduled for the next day would be cancelled.

At the Morgan Line, we were met by a considerable contingent of Yugoslav troops, which I was invited to review. I did this in company with Capt. John Blatnik, former president of the Junior Chamber of Commerce of Minnesota (and later to be chairman of the Public Works Committee of the U.S. Congress). He had just joined my office after several years of working with the partisans as a liaison officer, and was an ideal companion for a first trip across the line.

I found Abbazia to be the loveliest resort town I have ever seen in Europe. We registered at the Moskva (formerly Palazzo) Hotel, toured battered Rijeka (formerly Fiume), then gathered for dinner in a small nightclub adjacent to the hotel that was indistinguishable from the typical Hollywood drinking places of the post-prohibition era.

The cuisine, certainly, was more Italian than Slovene or Croat, and very good. Following the food and drink, my Yugoslav counterpart, Colonel Holjevac, made a little speech hailing our economic cooperation and expressing the pious hope that the same spirit of cooperation might be extended to political matters. In my reply, I ignored this invitation and contented myself with extolling the virtues of friendship and democracy, which I knew had a very different meaning for our hosts than it had for me and my colleagues. There was a bit too much drinking by all concerned, and for this and other reasons I decided not to stay the night; but it was a nice party while I was there and, I later learned, pepped up even more after my departure.

On a very different plane, but in equally friendly spirit, were my contacts and activities with the Boy and Girl Scouts. The scouts had been virtually abolished during the fascist era (replaced by the Young Fascists) and naturally there was no room for them during the German occupation. On September 16, pursuant to invitation, I attended a ceremony celebrating their reactivation. I wish I could say that the scouts in attendance represented a fair cross-section of the community; unfortunately, I cannot. I doubt that there was a single Slovene or Croat present. They saluted me with a precise and military snap that was not far removed from the gesture that Mussolini's appearance might have evoked a few years earlier.

Taking my cue from this and the obviously friendly countenances and attitudes I observed, I gave them a little speech, relating my own scouting activities as a war bond salesman, parader, Red Cross helper, and so on during World War I. From here, I adverted to the basic difference in concept between the fascist salute, connoting tribute or obeisance to a leader, and the scout salute as greeting to an equal. I even recited the scout oath, and told them that if everyone lived up to it there would be no more wars. The atmosphere throughout could not have been more cordial, and on many later occasions I again participated with the scouts in meetings and ceremonies.

Another project that had to be accomplished before the end of the summer was the organization of the Venezia Giulia Police Force.

When queried by the press as to the prime thrust of our mission in Venezia Giulia, I was accustomed to respond that our job was: "to feed, clothe, and house the people; to maintain public order, and to prevent disease and unrest, until the final disposition of the territory." Or words to that effect.

Following the war, feeding, clothing, and housing the people had presented few problems. Agriculture, disrupted by the war, was quickly resumed. If the food was not available locally, Uncle Sam was ready to bestow his largess on the whole world. The prevention of disease, as it turned out, never assumed the critical importance that it had early in the war in southern Italy. Maintaining public order and preventing unrest were obviously the prime priorities. Equally obviously, the prime instrument for the accomplishment of this objective had to be an efficient, dependable civilian police force.

Upon my arrival, General Harding informed me that considerable progress had been made toward this objective through the valiant and skilled effort of one of his 13th Corps staff officers, Geoffrey White, who had been a professional English policeman in civilian life. Using the British and other Commonwealth military police as a nucleus, White and his colleagues instructed them concerning the differences between military and civilian police jobs and standards, and then began the process of recruiting the large number of civilians who would be required to keep the peace under the special circumstances that existed. I was instructed to build on this and get on with the job as expeditiously as possible.

Italian police had been liquidated by firing squads, abduction, or flight. When the Yugoslavs seized control in May, they had organized the so-called Difesa Popolare (People's Defense) comprised mostly of partisans. Only a handful had police experience. Their duties had little relation to crime prevention. They had strolled the streets armed to the teeth, searching out fascists and others in disfavor with their masters. Rather than reassuring the people, their presence excited fear and alarm. By the most lenient standards, they were a hopelessly incompetent police force. They had to go.

Before my arrival, they had been assembled in a stand-down parade and required to hand in the arms they were carrying. Simultaneously, AMG police officers searched the barracks and recovered ten truckloads of rifles, tommy guns, pistols, grenades, and ammunition.

From that time, Zone A of occupied Venezia Giulia was without civilian police for more than three months, despite valiant effort. The reasons were various. Applicants for the police school that was set up soon after my arrival were threatened and manhandled by Slovene Communists determined to discredit an Allied Military Government. Proper equipment and uniforms were not to be had. Establishment of rates of pay and conditions of service had become tangled in red tape stretching from Trieste to Allied Force Headquarters far to the south.

Nevertheless, by late September a sufficient force had been trained in the elements of police work so that a start could be made toward preserving public order, both by diminishing the occasion and motivation for unrest by putting people to work, and by constituting a public safety force sufficient in size and adequately trained to suppress violence and disorders should they nevertheless occur. The Venezia Giulia Police Force, ultimately organized with a strength of five thousand men and women, had a profoundly beneficial effect. It absorbed from the labor market five thousand vigorous young people of all hues of the political spectrum. By putting them to work, it not only deprived them of any motivation to cause trouble, but actually forced them to join us (the British and Americans) as well as get acquainted with one another in a manner that local political and ethnic attitudes would not otherwise have permitted. At the same time, when fully organized and trained it provided a force capable of suppressing disorder when that became necessary.

But despite the valiant beginning that had been made, at the time of my arrival and for several months thereafter it could not be said that an effective civilian police force existed in the city. Notwithstanding my efforts, and partly because the new recruits liked it that way, the force was treated like a military unit until it was several months old. It was commanded by a British regular officer and not directly under my control. Once preliminary organization was completed, however, I had no trouble convincing my superiors that a police force, to be a proper police force at all, had to be subject to the control of the local civil government, which I, despite my uniform, headed at that time and place.

One of the first professional policemen to arrive in the territory, and thereafter the mainspring of all police activity in Venezia Giulia, was Maj. Gerry Richardson, later promoted to lieutenant colonel. He was a member of the Criminal Investigation Division of the London Metropolitan Police Force, which we Americans know as Scotland Yard. The colloquial designation for a plainclothes man or detective in English police slang is "finger," and because of his long association with this type of activity, the colonel was dubbed Finger Richardson. At our staff meetings, his report usually included the words, "Crime is satisfactory." To this day, I don't know whether or not he was joking.

When the Venezia Giulia Police Force was first organized, it was an integral military unit of the 13th Corps and had not yet assumed its permanent status as a part of civil (AMG) government. Consequently, it was deemed appropriate that its titular head should be a full line colonel. One was imported—a British regular army officer. A very pleasant chap, he was an officer and a gentleman in the best British tradition, but it cannot be said that he contributed very much to the force.

One contribution he sought to make but was prevented from so doing related to the police insignia and badge. Eventually the 13th Corps gazelle was settled upon, but not before the colonel had presented his alternative suggestion which, as God is my witness, he would have implemented without consultation had I not heard of it and alerted the corps commander. His idea for the badge was the official College of Arms crest of his own family. Seeking an appropriate occasion, General Harding persuaded him kindly that the idea was impractical. The colonel stayed on, however, until direct AMG command of the police was relinquished on April 1,

1946, at which time, after considerable discussion, it was decided that a nonprofessional should not head the force. Gerry Richardson took over completely, under my general direction.

As I have indicated, procurement of uniforms was a problem. Initially it was solved by dyeing American army uniforms, which became surplus as our soldiers went home. The color chosen was black. The only headgear available was the helmet liner (similar in contour to the hard hats worn by motorcycle policemen and other motorcyclists even today), and these were painted or enameled white. The typical Italian small wax match is black with a rounded white head and, in contradistinction to the *fiammifero* (or ordinary natural-wood kitchen match) is called a *cerino*. There was no denying the resemblance; there it was, the shiny white top on the slim black body. The locals called our policemen the *cerini*.

After a time, we got rid of the label by getting rid of the black uniforms and white helmet liners. There were good reasons for this, entirely aside from the derisive *cerini*. The uniform was too military in its general aspect, despite the black dye. This was misleading both to the beholder, perhaps about to be controlled, and to the wearer, who in many cases felt that being a soldier was more exciting or prestigious than being a policeman. I wanted to discourage this idea and to disabuse the police of any misconceptions about their military status.

In any event, as soon as it was possible, we got rid of the *cerini* aspect and the military look by adopting and fitting out our police with a blue uniform and helmet that closely resembled the familiar garb of the London Bobby. I made the selection myself, feeling that there was no other uniform in the world so generally recognized as designating a keeper of the peace, as distinguished from a soldier. The decision was greatly criticized at the time, particularly by American public safety officers—most of them policemen in their home towns—because it seemed, they thought, to play down American participation in public safety activity, which in fact was pretty sketchy at best.

One consequence of the uniform selection, which possibly I should have foreseen but did not, was that the uniform caused many of the local people as well as the world press and others (who should have inquired before reaching any such conclusion) to assume that the people who wore the uniform were, if not actually

London bobbies, then a force modeled closely after them and under sole British command. They were often referred to as British Police, which was somewhat unfair considering that everything they did was ultimately directed by this American. But I must say my British colleagues and superiors didn't seem to mind; possibly they rather enjoyed it.

I have said elsewhere that the Bora was an even more effective disperser of unauthorized demonstrations than a good heavy rainstorm. Third in order of effectiveness, in my experience from the time I was a Boy Scout and confronted the phenomenon in Detroit, is a well-trained, burly policeman astride a well-trained horse. There is something about the ominous clop-clop of a horse's hooves on pavement, as they draw closer and closer to the place where your toes are trying to stand their ground in the forefront of an unlawful assembly, that can cause the stoutest heart to quail.

It was for this reason (and not at all, as some traducers asserted, because I like to ride horses myself and it was nice to have a stable of them available) that we gave early attention to the recruitment, training, and deployment of a mounted corps, which was, indeed, from the beginning, fully as effective as I expected it to be. This was old hat for the predominantly British corps of Allied officers who had to do the job.

Much less congenial to their tradition was an idea quite novel for the time and place, although not at all unprecedented in other parts of the world: the female cop, or lady policeman as we called them in that more decorous day. They were seldom employed on riot duty, but were a splendid group of young women, intensely dedicated to their work. My local critics accused me of inspecting them more often than I did the rest of the force, and this may be true, although I tried to be impartial.

My Days and Evenings

*Reviewing a parade of the mounted element
of the Venezia Giulia Police Force*

My earlier reference to "the villa that had been requisitioned for me high on the hillside" was not exactly accurate. Nor do I wish to convey the impression that I was the first incumbent in the job I held for the next two years. Between June 12, the effective date of the Alexander–Tito settlement and July 4, when I arrived, it had been held by Col. Nelson Monfort, recently principal aide to Adm. Ellery W. Stone, the head of the Allied Commission in Rome. Nelson had been a longtime resident of Europe as an officer of a New York bank and was fluent in several continental languages. He was a very attractive man and my friend.

Before coming to Trieste, I had heard rumors that the reason he was departing was that he "couldn't get along with the British" in an area where, at that time, British personnel outnumbered Americans at all levels. I never asked Nelson and to this day do not know the facts in the case, but the concept of "getting along with the British" deserves a little attention for its own sake.

Whatever it took to get along was a talent with which I was apparently endowed by birth, supplemented by early experience. It had nothing to do with being subservient or agreeing on every point. In fact, anything that smacked of servility, or "going along" as distinguished from "getting along," was a sure road to contempt and loss of influence in decision making, which, in a totally integrated organization, necessarily involves a substantial element of consensus.

In my own case, I'm sure that the ease with which I learned to cope with British military manners, customs, and points of view had something to do with the fact that my father's family was Cumbrian by way of Essex and Kent. As a little lame boy born not long after the death of Victoria, I had been an insatiable reader of books by G. A. Henty, Rudyard Kipling, Charles Dickens, and a host of lesser British authors, with which my English grandparents' library was replete. My mother, the best thing that ever happened to my family before I married my wife, was of all-Irish descent, but patently believed that she had bettered herself by marrying an Englishman, though my father was at the time a shipping clerk who was never to set foot on British soil. I was affirmatively predisposed. I just *liked* these characters from the start.

In retrospect, I would be inclined to conclude that the fear or cultural aversion that many Americans felt for their British colleagues was attributable more to habits and manners than to any basic antagonism over military, moral, financial, or economic matters.

At the School of Military Government at Charlottesville, Virginia, in the spring and summer of 1943, one of my favorite lecturers had been a British officer named Travers Blackley, who had served with the Sudan defense force in 1940 and in the ensuing two years had been engaged in military government work in Ethiopia and Tripolitania. It was he who told of the horrifying test applied when circumstances required the execution of a native by way of reprisal under the International Rules of Land Warfare as they existed in those days. "We applied the aesthetic criterion," he told us. "When the identity of the real culprit could not be determined, we executed the ugliest of our captives." I never quite believed it, nor do I now.

I hope, though I can't be sure, that Colonel Blackley was pulling our legs; it would certainly have been easy to do. His academic audience consisted almost entirely of recently recruited civilians in uniform who were almost totally without background in the geographical and cultural milieus of his lectures. In any event, there can be little doubt that less shocking manifestations of a perceived or imagined British attitude toward "lesser breeds" did sometimes adversely affect social and operational interaction between American and Briton.

On the American side, the regular army officer assigned to military government duty was a very rare bird. In general, military government personnel were selected for special skills or qualities derived from civilian experience or background. For service in military government in Italy, the fact that proficiency in Italian was one such desirable skill resulted in the presence on the American side of many officers and enlisted personnel of Italian ancestry. Great Britain also contributed many basically civilian people, highly skilled in such technical fields as law, accounting, police work, and the like.

On the other hand, a considerable number of the nonspecialist British officers were regulars who had had many years of service in India ("pukka poona wallahs," other Britons called these) and other far away places with strange sounding names. While I yield to none in my admiration for the British officer corps, these were a special breed within that category. Closely related to them in the eyes of unsophisticated Americans were officers seconded from the Colonial Service. The racial orientation, social attitudes, and manners of some of these fine people were hard for the egalitarian Americans to swallow. Sometimes racial attitudes that were the natural result of their careers were reflected, in the early days in Italy, in a tendency to treat the local citizenry as natives, to the extreme displeasure of the Italian-Americans. Using monocles, tucking handkerchiefs up sleeves, carrying swagger sticks, and other un-American practices added to American alienation. When they called us "our late colonials" in jest, some of us weren't sure about that "late."

In discussing these matters, I speak as an American, although one who was at the time relatively immune to culture shock. I fully realize, and want it understood, that many American traits and practices must have been even more difficult for our British counterparts to tolerate. In any event, at the time of which I write, most of the more aggravating provokers of American discomfort had moved on to other places and duties, and lesser causes of irritation had become tolerable through familiarity on both sides. Still, the problem never entirely disappeared, and Nelson Monfort's release may have been one of its last manifestations.

For whatever reason, he had declined, or was discharged from, the duty I was about to assume. One thing Colonel Monfort did accomplish for me before he left was the requisitioning and whipping into shape for my occupation of the Villa Ina, or the Villa Schnabl, at 186 Via Romagna. High on a hill, it offered such an excellent view of the city and harbor that the occupant could, by standing on the terrace in front of his dwelling, ascertain visually whether a strike was imminent or a demonstration or riot about to break out.

I have said "Villa Ina or Villa Schnabl." Schnabl was the name of the owner, a businessman of Austrian or Swiss origin, who had decamped. When I moved in, his widow, Signora Schnabl, lived next door; she was happy to see me in possession and was a good neighbor for the next two years. Ina was, I was told, the good friend of Signor Schnabl, who had been the occupant of what was now my billet in the days before the war and, perhaps, for some time during the war.

Never mind, it was well chosen, not only for the strategic or operational advantages it offered, but as an almost perfect place to live and entertain. Built on a hillside, the lowest level was entirely undergound, the interior fitted like that of a British pub, or perhaps a German beer garden (I am more familiar with the former) with booths around the edges and dancing space in the middle. The second or main floor contained the kitchen, a dining room seating about ten or twelve people comfortably, and a spacious living room or parlor.

The third level provided sleeping quarters, with two bathrooms, one of which (mine, of course) was really a fully equipped small gymnasium, featuring what we now call a sauna, various rope and rowing devices for exercise at home, and a sun lamp with appropriate accompanying couch. In using the latter without adequate instruction in the early days of my occupancy, I became afflicted with violet ray burns of the cornea, resulting in considerable pain and requiring me to wear smoked glasses, which in turn necessitated embarrassing explanations. After a long war, I was obviously not prepared for la dolce vita!

This physical establishment was serviced by a full-time cook, a full-time waiter, and two maids. The only occupant other than myself was the young officer from time to time designated as my personal assistant (who would have been my aide de camp if I had been a general officer) except when that aide was a British junior commander (equivalent to a WAC lieutenant). When this was the case, for propriety's sake I took in another officer or civilian employee, male or female, to prevent the junior commander becoming another candidate for the title Colonel Bowman's Mistress. My Buick and Jeep (except when I drove the latter myself) were driven by military drivers who reported in the morning and served as needed, but lived elsewhere. If you think I lived well, you are right.

From this establishment, on a typical morning during the early part of my incumbency, I would depart sometime shortly after 7 A.M. for Duino Castle, headquarters of the British 13th Corps (whose only American staff officer I was) for the regular daily staff meeting, which took place at 8 A.M. This was usually short. Returning to my own headquarters in the Casa del Popolo at about 9:30, I met my own senior staff, heard their reports, and gave instructions for the day. The remaining morning hours were devoted to the study of problems, dictating replies to correspondence or orders for implementation, interviewing callers, or talking to members of the press.

This was the time when I accomplished most of the business I had to do that required personal contact or conversation, as distinguished from correspondence, planning, and the preparation of orders or instructions. The callers to whom I tried to give preference were the local, ostensibly nonpolitical ones—businessmen, labor leaders, and governmental officials. Visiting politicians from Great Britain and the United States also constituted a large segment of the persons I saw during this period. And, of course, there were the members of my own staff who required my views or action on matters either too personal or too detailed to be handled in the staff meetings.

In another room reached by a door behind me, slightly to the right of my right shoulder, sat my chief administrative officer, who took over the carrying out of agreements reached or instructions given, after the substantive problems involved had been resolved, either by agreement or my decision. Often the chief administrative officer would be called in to participate in the discussions, in order to avoid the necessity of later explanation.

The room in which I sat was a very large one, conceived and constructed in an earlier day of short-lived fascist grandeur and pretension. Between me and the door at the other end, guarded on the other side by my personal assistant and stenographer, was plenty of room for a gathering of twenty or more people. This was the area where the press conferences were held and where my guests, who sometimes came in planeloads, sat to hear me and others tell them what we were trying to do.

When the morning's business was finished, usually at about 1 P.M., I drove or was driven in my jeep (the upper reaches of the Via Romagna were too steep for the Buick, which was kept stabled at the Casa del Popolo) back to the villa for lunch—often with a visitor or a member of my staff. Following lunch, a half hour in the sun if the weather was good or a short siesta if I felt the need, I boarded my jeep with a companion and headed for the Caserma, where the police horses were kept. My companion was usually my personal assistant, male or female. In the latter case, inevitably, the poor girl would assume the character of the Slav mistress for an hour or two, since most of the good riding was in the Slovene-inhabited outskirts and she was a blonde. Sometimes my companion was a horse-loving visitor, and in the latter days of my time at Trieste I often took with me some or all of my adolescent children.

Following the ride and in observance of British custom long established in India and the tropics in the days before air conditioning, I returned to my office at about four and remained there, often completely alone (so far as I knew, but I suppose there was some kind of watch kept on my personal security) until about 7:30, when I drove or was driven up the hill for a short drink, dinner at about 8, and an evening either of reading or conversations with guests before usually early bed.

I might say that this was the usual but by no means the invariable routine, particularly as time went on and the situation either stabilized, or seemed to from time to time, or we had visitors who had to be entertained. Naturally, I was on all guest lists.

Every time a British or American ship of war called, there was likely to be a party of some kind—aboard if the ship were British, ashore if American because of the U.S. Navy policy against drinking on shipboard. Similarly, I was invited to all parties of enlisted men or other ranks, regiments as well as unit messes, British and American. I almost always sent regrets unless the affair had operational overtones, was a command performance (my attendance was expected by a superior), or would provide the occasion to meet and talk to an interesting person.

One of the honored guests in the latter category whom I remember best for an inconsequential reason was Gen. Mark Clark, fresh down from Austria, dressed in field uniform and chewing gum in the receiving line, with everyone else present dressed to the nines in his honor. Another was Ed Murrow, a great hero to the British as well as to his fellow Americans, for his radio broadcasts from a London hideout during the blitz. Field Marshal Montgomery was memorable because in his civvies, with watch chain stretched across vest, unexpectedly slight of stature, he was in appearance so unreminiscent of the black-bereted hero of Alamein.

The comedienne Gracie Fields and her escort or husband, an actor named Monte Banks, were another memorable pair, up from Capri where they had recently made their home. I loved Gracie, but Monte was a pain in the neck who had clearly come to the party with the idea that the head of the government was just the man to put the heat on for a couple of jeep tires. Not that the desire for jeep tires was unique. They were at that time literally the only kind of tires available, and people who could buy or steal them found ways to mount them on the most unlikely vehicles, such as long low Alfa-Romeos which, so fitted, scraped bottom every time they hit a slight bump or dip. In any event, I was not in the tire business and Monte didn't like me very much when the party was over.

There were other social occasions, of course, most of which I enjoyed more than the formal or informal military parties—perhaps because I was usually the central figure, and everyone likes attention. I refer to the dedications, village openings, fishermen's holidays, ship launchings, and other festivities, which are more fully covered in another part of this account.

From the beginning, I was the daily recipient of letters from the people and organizations of Trieste, addressed to me on a highly personal basis and concerning almost every subject under the sun. Many of these involved subjects I was not competent to deal with: for example, a plea by a group of ethnic Austrians for representation at the peace conference. Many petitioners begged for relief from injustice; persons deprived of employment because of their fascist background sought the opportunity to prove that they had never been even slightly sympathetic to fascism. I found it impossible to dispatch a military vehicle to central Italy to bring back the body of a soldier for the comfort of his pleading mother, but I did find a way to send an ambulance nearly as far to bear a very sick boy to a place where the surgery he needed could be skillfully performed.

Valerio Giorgi-Giurgevic urgently begged me to permit him to print and sell postage stamps for philatelic purposes, claiming the documented right to do so "on ground of the souverain [sic] rights recognized to the Haus of Giorgi-Giurgevic of which I am the Chief, by the former government of the Venetian Republic. My ancestors conquered by our own Army and Navy, 815 years ago, three big islands [off the Dalmatian coast] . . . where we reigned as Princes by the Grace of God from the year 1130 to the year 1433." A letter purporting to come from a number of dead persons buried in a mine in Istria contained instructions as to how to reach them, which I was requested to pass on to "our dear ones."

It was easy to grant the request of an ambitious student for a pass to go to Rome to apply to the British consul general there for the right to attend a British university. Messages that I was asked to deliver personally to President Truman and Foreign Minister Bevin were passed on in the direction of their designated recipients through the British and American political advisers. A way was found to help the people of Salona, who reported that a "bridge of the military type" (Bailey Bridge) was needed across the Isonzo in that locality because trucks carrying cement for the reconstruction of the village had been losing part of their loads due to the narrowness of the existing stone bridge.

These communications addressed to me on every subject under the sun were legion. Naturally, there was an element of flattery. I was "excellent," "illustrious," "egregious" (Webster left me in some doubt about that one), "esteemed," "genteel," and "exquisitely kind." They were self-respecting and without a trace of discourtesy to the addressee, no matter how unreasonable I must in some circumstances have seemed to the writers. This was true whether the writers belonged to the Italian or Yugoslav factions.

Another custom observed both in these letters and in the performance of local interpreters was the use of "Signor Colonello" both as a mode of address and in the third person. The best English equivalent either the interpreters or our staff translators of written material could come up with was "Mr. Colonel," which fails to reproduce the connotation of respect unquestionably intended by the speaker or writer. We are accustomed, in English, to address a very few functionaries in the second person, such as Mr. President, Mr. Speaker, or Mr. Chairman. So far as I can recall, however, justices of our appellate courts are the only officials to whom are applied the "Mr." preceding their functional titles, and even here only by lawyers and other judges. As a lover of both English and Italian, I always felt vaguely uncomfortable about Mr. Colonel, but of course there was nothing I could do about it.

The business involved in many of these letters to Mr. Colonel was, naturally, disposed of by subordinates. Those that really required my personal attention and action I customarily read on the road, while being driven to and from Duino Castle staff meetings or on other errands or missions outside the city. I had time to reflect on them, too, on such occasions, and to savor them, and think about their writers. And as I read there grew within me, despite the conflict and disorder all around, a genuine love for the writers and their fellow citizens of Trieste and Venezia Giulia.

Rank, Mistresses, and the Press

Media executives view Trieste from the terrace of the author's residence at 186 Via Romagna (U.S. Army Photograph)

Throughout my time in Trieste, I was customarily referred to in the press, both local and international, as the Governatore Militare Alleato or Allied Military Governor and during the past thirty years friends have frequently remarked about my command of "all those troops," referring to the totality of British, American, and other soldiers physically present in the area at the time. This concept greatly oversimplifies the command structure involved and tends to overrate my role in command terms.

According to established military doctrine, the military governor was in fact the theater commander, beginning with Sir Harold Alexander, followed by a succession of four- and three-star generals, including Americans Matt Ridgway and John C. H. Lee. My place in the military hierarchy was far down the line, as senior civil affairs officer of a British corps (containing an American division) whose primary function was to make sure that Tito did not march back in. From my position, I also looked up in another direction through channels to the Allied Commission in Rome headed by Reserve Rear Adm. Ellery W. Stone, who had almost complete discretion in military government matters in every other part of Italy. It was from this quarter that I obtained expert assistance and advice in various technical and professional aspects of the problems confronted, such as food supply, public safety, education, industry, and public works.

These diverse military superiors did not always see things in the same light. As a consequence, like many other military people on the working level before and after me, I found possibly the greatest challenge of my job in coordinating upward—pacifying and reasoning with my superiors along several divergent channels of command until I achieved a situation in which their orders were sufficiently harmonious to permit me to proceed and get the job done, whatever it might be. Downward, my power and discretion were absolute. Upward, they were subject to many restraints, some quite arbitrary, based on personalities or prejudice. Herein lay my greatest administrative problem.

As a practical matter, nevertheless, after some difficulties during the early months, I did indeed exercise all the primary powers of a totally unrestrained monarch. For whatever reason, my superiors in all the higher places to which I had to look for orders and guidance shortly seemed to acquire sufficient confidence in my judgment and actions so that I was left largely unfettered in the exercise of operational discretion. Sir William D. Morgan of Morgan Line fame at the time dubbed me King Bowman I of Trieste and so addressed me almost thirty years later when I last saw him in a fishing lodge in Scotland. He jested, but it is true that I was personally responsible for most day-to-day decisions made and actions taken.

As in any military government, let it be understood, these actions and decisions included all governmental functions that under the U.S. Constitution, and those of its component states, might be separately classified as legislative, executive, and judicial. The basic document establishing the policy and framework I operated under, and that would be supplied by a constitution in a democracy or republic, was Proclamation No. 1 of Field Marshal Alexander, the Mediterranean theater commander, promulgated on June 13, 1945, almost three weeks before my arrival. It declared the existence of the government I was to head, outlined certain offenses, and established courts to try them.

During the following three months, this basic document was augmented by six other proclamations dealing with such matters as property control, regulation of communications, temporary closing of financial institutions, establishment of a special court to try persons who had collaborated with the Germans after the Italian capitulation in September 1943, and dissolution of fascist organizations. Beyond this, through the promulgation of General Orders, orders of lesser application, administrative or otherwise, and Area Orders issued through the area commissioners of Trieste, Gorizia, and Pola, like any other military governor I made the laws, enforced them through police and other means, appointed the judges who tried their violators, and reviewed the sentences imposed by those judges. I was the law east of the Isonzo, as well as some points west.

My immediate superior in the area, the 13th Corps Commander Lt. Gen. Sir John Harding (later Lord Harding of Petherton) followed what I did closely and, on occasion, provided guidance with a firm hand but very light touch. At a later date in the occupation, speaking at a dinner in my honor, he told the company assembled that after long consideration he felt that my most prominent attribute was loyalty, up and down, the latter part meaning that I tended to defend the actions of my subordinates to a point sometimes beyond my own best interest.

If this was true, it is also true that I was the beneficiary of similar loyalty down from him, which he also on occasion carried beyond limits that self-interest might have imposed. On one occasion, for example (which I shall discuss at greater length later), I made an extremely unpopular, though sound, decision that attracted considerable adverse international attention from the world university community. After my dismissal of the beloved but pitifully incompetent (as an administrator) rector of the university of Trieste, there was an onslaught of press criticism. Yet General Harding announced the next day that this decision had been taken with his full knowledge and on his instructions. To this day, I have not the slightest recollection of ever having mentioned the matter to him. In fact, I am sure I had not.

Lord Harding may be the most remarkable man I have ever met as regards attributes of intelligence, courage, and leadership, but there were many other extremely exceptional people in the company in which I carried on my duties.

Within a few days after my arrival at Trieste, I was invited to attend a meeting that was intended to draw in, and pick the minds of, all concerned with civil administration and supply in northeast Italy. This included, of course, Brigadier John K. Dunlop, regional commissioner of the rest of the Three Venices, and me as the senior civil affairs officer, or regional commissioner, of the British–American-occupied portion of Venezia Giulia. It also included a host of officers from American, British, and Joint Headquarters and organizations, whose interest was involved only because demands would be made upon them for supplies or services of one kind or another.

The meeting was called, conducted, and presided over, by Gen. Sir Brian Robertson, head of administrative services for the theater and (in the words of Harold Macmillan, to which I subscribe) "the most efficient 'Q' (logistics) officer since Marlborough's Cadogan."

It was a democratic meeting, remarkably so, it seemed to me as it went on. All of us who had any ideas as to the best way to organize and to attack and solve the problems that confronted us were free to speak, and did so. There was a considerable spread in the opinions expressed, but after hours of discussion a palpable consensus emerged. At this point, General Robertson drew from his briefcase a paper several pages in length, obviously prepared by him long before the meeting was called to order, which exactly set forth the terms of the consensus. General Robertson was a remarkable man, and this was military leadership of the highest order.

The ensuing months were to provide contact with other military and administrative talent of as high an order as history has displayed. While I would place him slightly below Lord Harding (who had been his chief of staff) in basic qualities of leadership and intellect, there is no doubt that Field Marshal Alexander, who was at the top of the command structure in the Mediterranean theater at the time I assumed my responsibilities in Trieste and about to become Governor General of Canada, was one of the truly great personalities of our time.

During the early days at Trieste, both before the American division arrived and after, since the division was centered some distance away, as the senior American officer in the area and the only American on the corps staff, I was frequently paired with him at dinner and was tremendously impressed by his insights and perception. He had a way of understanding what I was going to say before I said it, which was disconcerting at the time but most impressive in retrospect. Like other great men, he was also a simple, direct person. Years later when I wrote him for advice about Canadian prep schools for my sons, the governor general replied at length, in his own hand. I last saw him shortly before his death when we bumped shoulders stooping to descry the price displayed on a bottle in the window of a liquor store in Shepherds Market in London's Mayfair. Though I had not seen him since 1950, Lord Alexander knew me at once. "Pretty awful prices, don't you think, Bowman?" he said as I introduced him to my wife. I never saw him again.

It was because I had early won the total support and confidence of men of this quality in high places that I appeared to the local populace, and to a degree to the world press, to be the source of all governmental action. Having explained this, I shall try not to refer to it again, but it should be understood that both my "we's" and "I's" in other portions of this narrative imply the participation of many persons who far outranked me.

In short, for all practical day-to-day purposes, in the eyes of the press and through the press in the eyes of the local people, I was the law giver, law enforcer, policymaker, and master of the region's destiny in the immediate future.

It was, of course, personally very satisfying and, in many respects, helpful in doing the job to enjoy the kind of confidence placed in me at Trieste—particularly when that confidence was bestowed by superiors of the high personal caliber of the general officers under whom I served at that time.

And, of course, one would be less than human if he did not enjoy being presented by the press and regarded by the people of the community in which he lives as the Lord High Boss of everything in sight. It requires constant reminders to oneself of Lord Acton's most prescient remark to Bishop Creighton on the tendency of power to corrupt but, once one is in charge of himself on this score, it is great fun.

However, there is another side to this matter of holding and exercising power. Inevitably, on the part of your adversaries or others who don't like what you're doing to them, it leads to attribution of all kinds of personal motives extrinsic to the job, which could be highly discreditable if true. In my case, one item sedulously cultivated and nourished by the local press was the myth of my mistresses—particularly the Slav one, who was most popular.

"Cherchez la femme" is a French proverb that receives full faith and credit in Italy. If you don't like what a man is doing—particularly a man in a place of power—look for the woman who is influencing his action. Since there was inevitably much that I did that was not locally pleasing to one faction or another, the mistress had to be invented by the press if she did not exist, as in this instance was the case.

Let me say that mistresses are indeed easy to come by in the military government business. Much has been written about this, some of it quite true. The combination of power and loneliness brings such relationships about, and the Italian and Venezia Giulia occupations saw the growth of many such relationships—some quite harmless over the long pull and others leading to tragedy for all or some of the parties concerned.

So, over a period of time, Colonel Bowman's mistress (who exercised through her charms complete control over his actions) either pro-Italian if you saw things from the Slav viewpoint or Slav if you were on the Italian side, was invented and reinvented by the press depending on which way things seemed to the inventor to be going for his side.

Two official intelligence reports submitted in September 1945 are pertinent.

> *From a pro-Italian source:* The supposed love life of Colonel Bowman is still one of the most-discussed subjects in town. The "Slav mistress" has been projected into a Hungarian secretary with additional functions of mistress, who is in reality a Slav and an OZNA agent. This would explain the alleged pro-Slav sympathies of the Colonel. The name of a certain Mrs. Mandic is often used as the name of one of the Slav lovers.

From a pro-Slav source: The supposed love life of Colonel Bowman is a frequent subject of conversation in Slav circles. A pro-Tito group claims that the Colonel has an Italian mistress of the Trieste aristocracy, and this would explain his pro-Italian and pro-reactionary attitude. The names of Cosulich and Parisi are frequently mentioned. The entire Tito group is positive that the Colonel has an Italian mistress, named Mara, who is a SIN agent.

Since there were more Italians than Slavs in the population, the Slav mistress was more frequently reported, and a blonde interpreter or receptionist would assume briefly a new, more glamorous, influential role. More often she was a creature manufactured from thin air and whole cloth. Sometimes she was a tragic victim, as in the case of the clerk in the Slovene bookstore down the street, as described in the following liberally translated excerpts from a Letter to the Governor.

> To: Colonel Alfred C. Bowman
> Trieste
>
> I am an Italian Triestino and a communist. This morning I entered the Slovene bookstore in the Corso only because I had seen one of my paintings displayed in the window, the property of the shop's owner. While I was looking at some books, the young lady clerk employed in the shop seeking comfort and advice, told me that she was being harassed by rowdy people who accused her of being Colonel Bowman's mistress although she has not ever even met him. These people, she said, open the door to the shop and shout "Petacci," the name of Mussolini's mistress. So you, Colonel, are compared to him! Several times while I was in the shop I saw youths peer in the door and laugh at the girl. So it is clear that the young lady is indeed the victim of a double calumny, which affects you as well, merely because she works in a store where Slovene books are sold. Before I left the store, she pulled aside the blind on a window facing the street, to show me the glass covered with spit! This is the renewal of fascism, Colonel. Take steps if you think best.
>
> > Giuseppe Moroj, Painter
> > via Scomparino 12
> > Trieste

I did not "think best," so long as no actual violence was involved. Anything I might have done would only have made matters worse. There were many such communications and much speculation in our free press on this subject, and by both sides. Despite a personal policy of totally avoiding all social contacts with locals of any persuasion except in a formal way in broad daylight with large numbers of people looking on, I was credited with a most amazing number of amatory liaisons with daughters, wives, and other personal representatives of everybody who was anybody on the local political and business scene. If the rumors had been true, what a life it would have been!

In this matter, as in all others involving newspapers and reporters, it was our policy throughout the occupation to permit virtually unlimited freedom of the press no matter how troublesome the result. It was particularly difficult to hew to this line when provocative and inflammatory stories in local papers unquestionably contributed to the unrest and occasional violence that it was our prime mission to keep in check. Only in cases of direct incitement to felonious violence did we ever interfere with press freedom, and then only to a very limited degree.

Historically, this policy has not commonly been followed in military occupations, particularly controversial ones. I would be hard put to explain how I got away with it, other than by referring again to the confidence with which my superiors honored me, perhaps augmented somewhat by their own personal preference for the libertarian way, a preference they might have been reluctant to confess to other professional military types.

I believe that I first proclaimed the policy at the press conference on September 1 with a quotation from Voltaire: "I disagree with what you say, but I will defend to the death your right to say it." Two days later, in somewhat milder language, I repeated the message to the public at large in two speeches delivered in Italian and Slovene. Each started with the same introductory words, although the speeches dealt with different issues. In each case, of course, I had the script of the speech prepared with the English words typed below the foreign ones, so that I could know what I was saying and add stress or expression to suit the subject matter. The Italian version was fairly easy. For eighteen months, I had been using the language for purposes of ordinary living, although never for official business without an interpreter; there was too much danger of wreaking havoc with one wrong word.

This is the way the script began in the Italian version, which was devoted to labor problems: *E' un principio fondamentale nei paesi liberi e democratici che le azioni del governo sono gli affari del popolo.* (It is a fundamental principle in free democratic countries that the actions of government are the business of the people.)

In the case of the Slovene speech, the problem was a little more complicated. The sound values of the letters of the Slovene words as they appeared on the script being totally unfamiliar, the script had to be prepared in three versions: (1) Slovene, (2) the Slovene version phoneticized in terms of English sound values, and (3) the English version, thus:

Slovene V Demokratichnih svobodnik dezelah velja nacelo, da je vlada za zvoya dejanja odgovorna ljudstvu.

Phoneticized oo demo<u>krat</u>ichnee svo<u>bod</u>nee dez<u>he</u>la velya nachello da yeh vlada za zvoya de<u>han</u>yah oudgo<u>vor</u>nah <u>lied</u>stvoo.

English It is a fundamental principle in free democratic countries that the actions of the government are the business of the people.

Educated readers fluent in the Italian or Slovene tongues, or both, will doubtless find some imperfections of punctuation, grammar, or syntax in the above lines, but I must be honest. These excerpts were copied directly from the sheets of paper from which I read my broadcast messages.

On the whole, the speeches went over well in both languages. However, I was not altogether successful in my use of the phonetic script. Despite my best effort, some of the accents of the foreign language I knew best crept into my delivery in a language I did not know at all. The communist and Slovene language press reported the following day that I spoke Slovene with an Italian accent. Since this was not good for the business I was in, during the rest of my term as governor I was prevailed upon to speak in Slovene on very few occasions indeed.

From the beginning, the most gifted, imaginative journalists were two students at the University of Trieste who published a satirical journal that at various times bore the mastheads *Caleidoscopio* or *La Cittadella*. For journalistic purposes, these two called themselves Angelicus and Ruben, and although I came to know their real names and to enjoy their friendship to the greatest degree compatible with my duties, I shall so refer to them whenever occasion requires in the pages to follow.

In the year following my departure, Angelicus and Ruben incorporated some of the more amusing passages about me and my regime from *Caleidoscopio* and *La Cittadella*, along with some new connecting passages, into a volume entitled *Sotto Due Bandiere, Tre anni di storia antipatica*, edited by F. Zigiotti. It was published only in Italian, but I was able to translate some of its more promising passages into English. In one of these, using some of the characters and the style of John Steinbeck's *Cannery Row*, my favorite local critics contrived an interesting theory about my antecedents and qualifications for the office to which I had been assigned:

> Out in California, one day, Attorney Bowman had defended the paisanos when Pilon had set fire to the house of The Greek. The grateful Pilon had presented him with a copy of *The Modern California Encyclopedia*, stolen, naturally, from the priest. From this volume Bowman had acquired all his learning about Trieste. He knew that at Trieste there was the North Wind (Bora), a port, the Miramare Castle, and as throughout Italy, lots of fascists.
> On the train, he had been told that there were also Slavs.
> "How many?" he had inquired.
> "Depends," they had answered him.
> Bowman, to be on the safe side, had concluded that if, after all the frightful fascist repressions of which he had heard, *any* Slavs were still alive and stirring, their number must have been at least half the total population. These, according to us [Angelicus & Ruben] are the mythological antecedents of Colonel Bowman's arrival at Trieste.

Although I did not arrive in Trieste by rail, my student friends did not greatly overstate the case. It was true that I had been a lawyer in Detroit and Los Angeles before the war, although my practice had inclined toward real estate and probate. I had practiced criminal law for a few months only as a deputy city attorney, and then on the prosecuting side.

Nor were they very wrong as to the extent of my special knowledge about the local problems of Trieste when I arrived there. My training at the School of Military Government two years earlier had certainly not highlighted Trieste as a special problem. For the intervening two years, I had known of it only as the part of pre–World War II Italy that prior to World War I had for several hundred years been part of Austria. I had heard that Field Marshal Alexander and Marshal Tito had agreed earlier in the year that when they met, presumably at Fiume, both British-American and Yugoslav forces would wheel north toward central Europe where, as projected, the Germans would still be resisting. For purposes of administration, Venezia Giulia was just one of the three major subdivisions of the region of Venice.

Why, then, was I selected for this critical post, involving millennia of conflict between races, nationalities, and ideologies? A good question. The military generally cherish and apply the concept of the good man as distinguished from the man of specialized knowledge. Presumably they considered that since I had done well in my last previous assignment despite similar ignorance of local factors, I would do well in this one. I have myself often followed this rule in selecting a subordinate. I hope that history—using the term in a very modest sense—has proved that the theory had merit.

Throughout my incumbency, day to day, week to week, and year to year, the local and international press was possibly the most important single force I had to deal with. This was a fairly new experience for me. I had conducted some press conferences in Bologna, but they had been attended almost exclusively by local reporters from the Italian press, who at that time were polite to the point of being obsequious in the presence of Allied military authority. At that time, the attention of most of the world press was focused on northern Europe, although I remember that cartoonist Bill Mauldin had dinner in our mess on the evening of the day the war in Europe ended.

In Trieste, the situation was very different. The first encounter was on July 16, about twelve days after my arrival, when a planeload of journalistic stars descended for a conference devoted to the matter of some arrests of communists that had taken place before my arrival. This had been a military action unrelated to military government per se, and the truth is that I knew nothing about the arrests and had to say so. Not a very good beginning, although I remember there were a few compliments about the openness and frankness of my attitude and manner. Cy Frieden of the *New York Herald-Tribune* and Phil Hamburger of the *New Yorker* were among those present. It was a heady experience for me to have twenty by-line British and American reporters fly in for the single purpose of hearing what I had to say and then fly out after I had said it.

It may be taken for granted in other portions of this account, from beginning to end, that the goings-on in Trieste drew a multitude of reporters from the outside, some of whom remained for considerable periods of time, or returned frequently. I have mentioned Cy Frieden and Phil Hamburger. Cy at times seemed about to become a permanent resident. There was another Cy, C.L. Sulzberger of the *New York Times*, whose Camille Cianfarra, James "Scotty" Reston, the redoubtable Anne O'Hare McCormick, and Herbert Mathews also appeared frequently. Sidney Koreman of the *Chicago Tribune* was another old resident who became a close friend and occasional adviser, to the degree that his advice was compatible with the essentially adverse relationship between news gatherer and news subject.

Among others who honored us with considerable attention were Barrett McGurn, then of the *New York Herald-Tribune* and now director of public information for the U. S. Supreme Court, and James Wellard of the *Chicago Times*. Our conferences were unstructured and, on any given occasion, there were likely to be several correspondents present whom I had never seen before and would never see again. By and large, they were a fine bunch of people.

This was also a time when many amateurs used their prestigious names to get into the business of being foreign correspondents. Prominent in this category was Randolph Churchill, son of the great Winston, who used Trieste as a base for forays into Yugoslavia. Another was Doris Duke, clearly selected for her name value but a young woman with a photographic memory. She interviewed me one day for more than two hours taking no notes whatsoever, yet the resulting INS article could not have more accurately reported what I told her. Another slightly different category of newsman was the politician who wrote for the press as a sideline. Maurice Edelman, a member of the British parliament, was an eminent representative of this class, who wrote for the *Picture Post* of November 3, 1945, as letter-perfect a summing up of our problems (albeit with a slight slant to the left as befitted a Labour Party member) as any full-time professional ever did during my time in Trieste.

Then there were the stringers. I shudder at the memory. For the uninitiated in press terminology, a stringer is a reporter who is not a salaried employee of any publication, but goes out on his own to find newsworthy stories, for which he is paid by the word, line, or page. Recognizing that the word is sometimes used in a somewhat broader sense, for the purposes of the observations I am about to make this character (and some of them are very worthy people in all other respects) is a reporter who is not paid unless he is published.

It is obvious that when a member of this club is hungry, the temptation to fabricate, aggravate, or incite, that is, create news, can be overwhelming. One stringer who comes to mind spent much time in Trieste, traveling with his wife who was also a reporter. I liked them both; aside from our professional relationship, we were friends. Despite this fact, they concocted out of whole cloth and kitchen door rumors a massive cock-and-bull story that the Soviet fleet was sailing full steam toward Trieste in battle formation via the Sea of Marmora and the Dardanelles. The story was actually distributed to the American press by a national wire service and could have started a new war. At the time, these people were restrained to a degree in the exercise of perverted imagination (in other words, lying in print) by libel laws and the fear that, when the chips were down, they might be held accountable. I tremble when I think what might happen against the national interest now that they, along with their more secure salaried colleagues, are immune in most places from the obligation to disclose the sources of such stories; in effect, they now have the "right" to lie.

Another way to get a story in order to avoid going hungry, of course, is not to make it up but to make it happen by creating an incident. A favorite forum for this sort of thing was my regular press conference, at which I made statements to and answered questions from both local and world press representatives. The American or British stringer could and would take advantage of these occasions, which otherwise were a splendid instrument for improving our local relations and winning press cooperation in our programs, by calling one of the local reporters a liar or making some remark about his personal life, or questioning his motives, or attacking his ethnic background or politics.

The purpose, of course, was to evoke a newsworthy reaction in the yellow journalism sense, producing a headline such as "Slav Reporter Strikes U. S. Correspondent," "Trieste Newsman Says AMG Lies," or something of the sort. Actually, this never worked. The local reporters, recognizing the stringer's motives, refused (with my moral support and thanks for their restraint) to rise to the bait. Still, it remains my view more than thirty years later that the stringer is a menace to the public weal and to world order and should be abolished by a constitutional amendment if the press will not do the job itself.

A prime requisite for a successful press conference that includes correspondents and reporters who speak different languages is, of course, a competent interpreter. In the case of my conferences in the Casa del Popolo, this meant one who spoke both Italian and English. For some reason, even the most zealous ethnic protagonists of the "Slovene littoral" theme never suggested that any of the local journalists who attended the conferences could not understand or make themselves understood in Italian. So we never had to translate twice.

As anyone with extended experience dealing with interpreters must have learned, they come in three categories. The one I prefer is what might be called the G. I. type, who is probably an American by birth and who, using the first person, as if he were the person speaking or responding, translates word for word, perhaps not having the slightest idea what the original speaker is trying to get across. I had become accustomed to this type during the war. The second category is the indigenous civilian of some education who tries to emulate the G. I. type, but can't quite make it because of his local background. Nevertheless, he tries hard and does a pretty good job, marred only by the interjection of local phrases like *non e vero?* (isn't it so?; which is equivalent to the present day "y'know"). His great disadvantage is that he is sometimes a little short on vocabulary to express ideas that will link speaker and listener if properly expressed. The third is the highly educated, thinking type, who offers advantages in vocabulary but has the weakness of constantly tending to embroider or extend or explain what the speaker says.

One of Trieste's prime claims to distinction was that it had been, for an extended period between wars, the home of the great James Joyce, who earned his living there by teaching English while he began writing his masterpiece *Ulysses*. During my time in Trieste, his brother Stanislaus, later author of *My Brother's Keeper* but then a professor at the university, was still on hand.

After I had been unable to locate a qualified G. I.-type, and my local, while very willing, had proved inadequate for some occasions, Professor Joyce became my press conference interpreter for the balance of my tenure. He was an erudite and gentle man and never at a loss for the right Italian word to convey the meaning of my pronouncements. Nor do I remember any of my press inquisitors ever having claimed to be mistranslated. However, he was also the quintessential type three who, instead of using my words, drifted into a pattern of telling my audience in his own words the gist of what I had said, sometimes even of what I thought, even though this thought could only be adduced from the context of what I had said. Still, his talents and erudition outweighed the disadvantages of these academic habits and, on the whole, I was very lucky to have him.

I have often been asked, both while this was going on and during the years that followed, why I didn't simply study Italian and learn to answer the questions of the press in that language without an interpreter, as Regional Commissioner Charles Poletti (I was told) had done in Naples, Rome, and Milan. As a matter of fact, I had during the preceding eighteen months necessarily learned enough of the language to be able to look after my own living needs while traveling, to give orders to servants at home, and the like. Why not indeed?

There was an obvious reason, applying particularly to Venezia Giulia, of course. Bowman the speaker of Italian would have become Bowman the Italian in the Slovene press. Perhaps I could have lived with that. Other reasons, applying anywhere when delicate or critical matters are involved, are more important.

First, even within one-language nations like Italy, the signification of words can often vary markedly between communities. A word harmless in context in Rome, may be offensive or misleading when used in similar context in Bologna or Trieste. Serious misunderstanding may result. Second, when a statement is misunderstood and becomes controversial it is, as a practical matter, useful to be able to blame the misunderstanding on the interpreter, even if the speaker himself is in fact to blame—a cowardly but practical consideration. Third, and perhaps most important, if one knows enough of the language to grasp the thrust of the inquiry or accusation as it is originally expressed, the translation gives one time to compose a well-rounded, responsive answer or comment that might not be forthcoming under conditions of stress and immediacy. Many years later, when I was chief staff-level negotiator at Panmunjon following the Korean War and all questions and answers had to be translated twice (into Chinese and Korean, in the case of an American respondent), I found this consideration even more critically important than it had been in Venezia Giulia.

The principal indigenous newspapers of Trieste were the Italian communist *IL Lavoratore*, the Slovene communist *Primorski Dnevnik*, and the left wing *Il Corriere Di Trieste*. None was favorably disposed toward Allied Military Government. Even though AMG had given them freedom of the press for the first time in 25 years, criticism and abuse dripped from the editorial pens.

To give the people a less biased, more factual presentation of the news, the Allied Psychological Warfare Board (PWB), later renamed Allied Information Service, and commanded by the highly able and dedicated Col. Douglas M. Street, sponsored an Italian-language daily, *Giornale Alleato*, and the Slovene-language *Glas Zaveznikov*, first published on June 19, 1945.

The *Giornale Alleato* was an immediate success, and although distributed in the afternoon, it outsold all its competition. Later, *La Voce Libera* was published, expressing a more conservative, pro-Italian viewpoint.

If newspaper circulation is any criterion, the population of the city of Trieste in 1945 was about 85 percent Italian (census figures of 1921 show 90 percent) and politically to the left, but not communist. Noncommunist papers outsold communist dailies three to one.

Government and Schools

Slovene school reopening

As the summer of 1945 waned, it was necessary to confront another critical problem created by the provision of the Duino Agreement, signed at Duino Castle on June 20, which required that we use "such elements of the existing Yugoslav administration as may be working satisfactorily."

While their zealous comrades were settling old scores in other parts of the zone, the local members of the Yugoslav command had undertaken to remodel the existing traditional machinery of civil administration. Prefects and *sindacos* (mayors) had been dismissed, and the government process placed in the hands of the National Committee of Liberation, which had been formed in 1944 as an underground organization dedicated to freeing Venezia Giulia from both German and Italian domination. I learned that the personnel constituting the committee when I took over had been freely elected by acclamation at an assembly convened in the 2,500-capacity Politeama Rosetti Theater in Trieste, at which the candidates had been presented and proposed by the Yugoslav military authorities.

The regular Italian police forces had been dissolved, and the prisons emptied. Many of the prisoners gladly reversed roles on the spot and joined the Difesa Popolare, the Yugoslav civil police force. A so-called People's Court had been established to dispense justice to persons who were so fortunate as to have been only arrested and not removed to other places by the Difesa Popolare.

As one of my officers expressed it at the time, the governmental machinery that evolved from this process had "a loud horn, but no motor." It purported to be a sort of pyramid of administrative committees, topped by the National Committee of Liberation. The lower echelons—the district and commune committees called the *consulta* and the *assemblea*—were said to have been elected locally by free vote of the inhabitants in each community.

Inquiries I caused to be made revealed that these asserted local free elections had all been conducted in a manner similar to the elections of members of the National Committee in Trieste, in hastily convened public assemblies by acclamation, not secret ballot. Since they took place in May, during the Yugoslav occupation, it would have been surprising if the bodies so elected had not been dominated by supporters of the then-occupying power.

Since the terms of our commitment were to use such elements of the existing Yugoslav administration as might be found to be working satisfactorily, the mode of election might have been regarded as irrelevant if the resulting structure had been effective for governmental purposes. Many of the persons elected were indeed dedicated anti-fascists and had been active partisans on our side in the bloody fight to overthrow Mussolini and Hitler. By and large, however, they were not even slightly trained in administration or competent to handle the reins of government. Often they were arbitrary, dogmatic, domineering, utterly unable to compromise. It became increasingly evident to me very early in my incumbency that they were incapable of effectively conducting the routine, essential business of government.

It was equally evident, as time went on, that the personnel who constituted the Yugoslav-installed bodies would not voluntarily relinquish their authority and asserted prerogatives. This caused me to initiate late in July an accelerated study to determine the best way to remedy the deficiencies and get local government back on the track.

The study process generally preceded the issuance of a General Order and was conducted by my staff officers. Since most of them had worked earlier under senior officers of the Allied Commission for Italy or at Allied Force Headquarters, I had to assume they would seek advice from these sources. But to this day, I do not know how much consultation of this kind actually took place.

I do know, however, that General Order No. 11, which emerged from this particular staff study and was possibly the most controversial one I ever signed, was not influenced in any way by pressure from above. The reason I can be certain is that in the course of completing this book I talked with Dr. Ralph Temple who, as a major on the staff of the Allied Commission, did most of the spadework on General Order No. 11. He assured me that his recommendations to me at that time, while conforming generally to an earlier directive of Allied Force Headquarters concerning local government, were based strictly on his own observation of needs and conditions in Venezia Giulia and were in no way influenced by instructions or suggestions from his base. (Major Temple's report on local government organization in Venezia Giulia, July 1945, appears in the Appendix.)

I can only conclude that if no command pressure through staff channels was exerted in this most controversial instance, the probabilities are slight that it was imposed in any other case. In short, I was given the latitude to base my actions on my own judgment and discretion.

General Order No. 11 was published on August 11 and entitled "Local Government." It divided the zone into three areas comprising the portions of the former provinces of Gorizia, Trieste, and Pola that were now under our control. It provided for presidents and councils to be appointed by Allied Military Government, not only for these areas but for the communes into which they had historically been divided.

The real heart and most important part of the order, however, was compressed into two pregnant sentences; one was in Section

10: "No committee, council, or group other than those herein created and provided for, except those previously constituted by a proclamation or order of the Allied Military Government, shall possess any of the administrative, legislative, executive, or other powers of government."

The other was in Section 11: "Allied Military Government is the only government in those parts of Venezia Giulia occupied by the Allied Forces and is the only authority empowered to issue orders and decrees and to make appointments to public or other office."

However sensible my motives and unavoidable the action taken, the order naturally constituted a severe blow to the plans of the partisans and the local Slovene minority. Reaction came quickly. In Trieste the Communists held a parade, ostensibly to celebrate the end of the Japanese war, actually to demonstrate against Allied Military Government. Marchers carried slogans proclaiming:

Long live Italo-Slovene Brotherhood

The Giulian region is not an enemy country

We want the Atlantic Charter to be applied

Their energies expended in songs and shouts, the paraders went home. No one was hurt. Four days later, on August 19, the Italians responded with their own "V-J Day" procession and celebration. Some pro-Yugoslav youths attacked the parade, and street fighting started, but order was restored within two hours by American and British military police.

At Pola, trouble between the Italian and Croat residents anticipated by several days the actual publication of the order rumored to be on the way. When Field Marshal Alexander visited the former Italian naval base on August 4, the Italian activists seized the opportunity to let the world hear the voice of the theretofore-cowed ethnic majority. They arrived first on the scene in the public square where he would appear and gave him a tumultuous welcome.

Arriving a bit later, the opposition—mostly Croats with a few Italian Communists—lined up on the opposite side of the square to hurl insults and epithets. When a few excited Italian teenagers attacked their tormenters, the military police ordered everyone to go home. The Italians obeyed, but the Communists remained to engage in a melee with the MPs that reached dramatic proportions before police reinforcements arrived to turn the tide. In the end, 21 of the troublemakers were jailed for breach of the peace, assault, and resisting arrest.

Later, on August 23, the same dissident group demonstrated specifically against General Order No. 11, but the first fine careless spirit was gone, the parade was tepid, half-hearted, and passed without incident.

The demonstrations were the most palpable, but not the most critical, aspect of the opposition to General Order No. 11. In every communist-controlled commune, implementation was impeded if not prevented. In a letter to me dated September 6, Dr. Bevk, the head of the National Committee of Liberation (CLN), warned me that his organization would not cooperate with Allied Military Government under General Order No. 11 because it established a system of government "fundamentally not different from the fascist system of public administration," because "AMG cannot base the General Order No. 11 upon International Law," and because cooperation would be a breach of faith with the people by whom they (the CLN members) were elected. Following Dr. Bevk's lead, Slovene doctors, lawyers, judges, technicians, and others who had previously agreed to accept government positions withdrew their support. In some communes opposition was passive; in others there was open defiance. At Turiacco, an Italian village, the communist leader shouted to the people, "Go into Monfalcone and form a new Council, and when you return we will come in and cause you to disappear, one by one." In Monfalcone the Communists posted an appeal to the citizenry:

Citizens of Monfalcone:

The decisive day of Victory over the International armed fascism should have been a day of rejoicing for all of us. But it is not so. Our popular power has been deprived of its authority by AMG. We have been deceived. We should fight, and secure at last the form of government for which we yearn. We gave all for Liberty's sake. Now we demand respect for our sacred right to liberty, won by hard struggle.

Long Live democracy. Long Live Truman. Long Live Attlee. Long Live Tito. Long Live Stalin.

In Gorizia, also, there was a wave of lawlessness. In his monthly report for September the Area Commissioner said,

> Armed bands have terrorized country people at night. Landowners have been driven from their farms and threatened with violence if they return. The people of Gorizia city, mostly Italian, have asked to arm and patrol the streets for protection during the late hours of the night. The Italians, tired of their law-abiding role and of abuses and threats, have now openly threatened reprisals.

The Gorizia Communists held their V-J Day parade on August 17, tearing down Italian flags and molesting Italian girls.

In the end, it proved infeasible to enforce General Order No. 11 fully according to its terms in the more remote and recalcitrant communes. Often, no one could be prevailed upon to serve as president in the absence of effective police protection, which we were not at that time able to furnish, since there were as yet no civil police, and military police could not be employed for this purpose. Immediate forced implementation being impossible, I instructed my officers to eschew firearms, use persuasion and diplomacy so far as these could be effective, and beyond that to do the job without help if necessary. We were, after all, a provisional, temporary government, whose prime mission was to maintain peace pending final disposition of our temporary domain. It was better, I concluded, to accept half a loaf, than no bread.

Eventually, the scheme worked pretty well, although in some of the more difficult places the civil affairs officer constituted for practical purposes the whole government for the full duration of my time. Thus, for the first time in Europe under Allied Military Government, complete military rule existed de facto. In the recalcitrant communes, unlike the situations in the conforming ones (of which there were many), the CAO did not advise or supervise the mayor; he *was* the mayor. It was a challenging assignment for one individual, especially for someone who was foreign to the system. Yet I am sure the dedicated men who performed it would have been reluctant to pass up the experience.

Even while prime attention was directed toward the problems of re-establishing local government on a workable basis, it was necessary to confront and deal with another imminent matter that was likely to cause as much heartburn on the Italian side of the community as General Order No. 11 had done on the Slovene/

communist side. It was now August. School-opening time comes in September in Trieste and the rest of Venezia Giulia. And in Trieste then, as in Canada and California now, there was the question of bilingual education.

Bear in mind that this was Italia Irredenta, redeemed less than three decades before from centuries of domination by an empire whose populace included many Slavs and Germans. Under Mussolini's regime, the very thought of Slovene schools or instruction in the Slovene or Croat languages would have been very close to treason. The resident Slavs had several options, all of them directed to the desirable end of becoming cultural Italians.

Considering the problem in the perspective of our status as mere stakeholders pending an undetermined and undeterminable future that might see Venezia Giulia awarded either all or in part to either Italy or Yugoslavia, or to neither of them, the proper course seemed obvious. Clearly, we should permit each student to prepare for adult existence within the nation he hoped would prevail. In the face of a tide of Italian resentment, we decided to provide education in the Slovene language and about Slovene concepts and traditions for those children whose parents wanted it.

Some of the problems involved in opening the Slovene-language schools were present in equal degree in the case of the Italian schools. One of these occurs everywhere, in every war, where towns are occupied. It is a military secret known to every officer and most enlisted men that schools make excellent ready-made barracks. They are almost ideal, with sanitary facilities, spacious rooms, lockers, and all the other things soldiers require for comfort and efficiency. Venezia Giulia was no exception. Thousands of soldiers had been comfortably put away in schools, and some of their officers as well. They had to be ousted—often to less comfortable quarters. It was not easy to arrange in all cases.

Another problem was that teachers of all ethnic and political persuasions seemed to have been more anxious than other citizens to flee the area when the Yugoslavs and British/American forces had come in. They had to be rounded up and brought back. Fortunately, we were able to offer them better pay and working conditions than prevailed either in Yugoslavia or in Italy at this point in history. The mission was accomplished.

Opening the Slovene schools was not an easy task in other

respects. We discovered that the Committees of Liberation set up by the Yugoslavs in May were requiring prospective Slovene teachers to appear before them for screening and indoctrination before applying to AMG for jobs. Pressure was also brought to bear to have each applicant appointed to a post selected by the committee. Parents were importuned to write AMG requesting the appointment of the teacher selected for their district by the Committee of Liberation.

As a gesture of goodwill, we asked the Committee of Liberation to help find suitable textbooks, which were promised and delivered in due course. They were very colorful and very instructive. From them, children were certain to learn of the glory of Tito and of the wonders of communism and very little else. Obviously, we couldn't use them. To their eternal credit, and with incredible courage considering the conditions under which they had to do it in remote villages almost under the visual scrutiny of disgruntled partisans and CLN adherents, the Slovene teachers themselves buckled down with typewriters and mimeograph machines to turn out the alternative Slovene-language textbooks that would be needed to carry on their work.

Despite these difficulties and many more, Italian and Slovene schools opened in Venezia Giulia on the announced date, October 16. Children were learning reading, writing, and arithmetic in the languages they spoke at home. And the same people who had been so critical of our action in promulgating General Order No. 11 grudgingly admitted that in this instance, perhaps, the point of view of the interested but uninvolved military administration under which they temporarily had to live was sound. There can be no doubt that this slight concession to the Slav presence took much of the remaining steam out of the anti-11 protests.

The end of a long and hectic month devoted to the amelioration and control of the disorders that followed the publication of General Order No. 11 happened to coincide with a meeting in Trieste attended by the British ambassador Sir Noel Charles and Field Marshal Alexander, on his way back to England to receive His Majesty's commission as governor general of Canada.

On the day before the arrival of these notables, I had received an uncharacteristic message from the Allied Commission, in effect asking my views as to what should be the permanent solution of the political-ethnic problem presented by the disputed territory of which I temporarily had charge. This seemed to me to present a clear conflict with my function as impartial low-level trustee. The stakeholder, I thought, should not also be asked either to testify or to judge. Nevertheless, the query had caused me to give the matter some thought.

As was his custom, the field marshal, the most simple and direct of men, asked me what my problems were—particularly those of an administrative nature. As it happened, the prospective immediate loss of American officers under criteria that made most of them eligible to return home at once was foremost, although I felt many would stay if their families could join them. Alex (as we affectionately called him when out of his presence) noted my points in a little black book, then asked me the same question put to me by the Allied Commission a few days before that had been haunting me ever since.

I am not sure that later on, out from under the pressure of the hectic events of the preceding month, I would have given the same answer; but, in fact, I did reply that I could see no feasible solution other than a free state of some kind under the control of the United Nations. I shall never know, nor do I want to, whether my words (also noted in the little black book) had anything to do with the fact that the free territory idea permeated the discussions of the foreign ministers that began in London on September 20. The fact is, in any event, that the idea germinated early, before any of the surveys and official visits that occurred later, ostensibly to enable the foreign ministers to make an objective decision.

It may be worthy of note that following an assembly of teachers during early October, which I addressed and during which I was treated rudely by some of the teachers present, I received a note of apology for the behavior of these people from one of their colleagues, who then went on to say:

> I certainly would not presume to offer political advice to an authority of your stature. What is more, on the part of a woman this would be very counterproductive, not only as presumption on my part as your guest but because political women always manage to be insupportable. Nevertheless, I shall express to you my idea, which is also that of many Giulian people of good sense. The Trieste problem would be resolved by the constitution of a Giulian independent state, which would allow the pacific cohabitation of the two people whom nationalism now makes antagonists, and would also help the economic situation and promote collaboration between the two interested nations for reasons of a geopolitical nature.

Whether these views were in fact those of "many Giulian people of good sense," I shall never know. In the thirty-odd years since all these things happened, I have been assured by others that this was indeed the case, but even those who so assure me have refused to identify themselves as holding the view stated. The more honor, then, to the woman who wrote to me and signed her name to what she wrote.

As the month ended, I found some comfort in a press-reported response by the British under-secretary of state, Philip Noel-Baker, to a question put to him in the House of Commons about the situation in Trieste. He replied that part of the population had shown some reluctance to collaborate with us, but that up to that point no serious incident had taken place. He added that he was glad to be able to assure the House that the Allied authorities had shown tact and skill in the handling of their difficult task.

I was happy to settle for that appraisal.

Prelude to Decision

Pro-Slav demonstration, May 1, 1946

The Council of Ministers of Foreign Affairs of the Big Four nations met in London from September 11 to October 2, 1945. Almost immediately, the word was whispered that the disposition of Venezia Giulia would involve something in the nature of a free state. There were also immediate rumors that the foreign ministers themselves would come to Trieste to seek evidence at the grass roots. However, this did not happen, and it was almost five months before anybody of official consequence came to evaluate the situation on the ground. At least this diminished concern about possible super-demonstrations, ostensibly proving something about the will and ethnic character of the locals who were bound to meet any delegation from the United Nations or any of the Big Four nations, and gave me time for other problems.

Prominent among these was the loss of American officers. The army had devised a scheme, which entitled them to be released and sent home, based on varying degrees of credit for service in various places. Most of my officers had been in Italy for almost two years, following service in the United States and elsewhere, which, in the aggregate, entitled them to go home at once.

Still, these were dedicated experts, men of high quality who had enjoyed and felt a sense of mission about the work they had been doing since the invasion of Sicily or earlier. I am satisfied that had the Army offered them anything specific in the way of opportunities for promotion, home leave, reasonable terms of continued service, and a commitment of some sort concerning the prospects of being joined by their families, many would have stayed. Of course, some, including me, stayed anyhow; but my case was not exactly typical and I did have some informal assurances about home leave and the possibility of my family's joining me.

In any event, the necessary assurances were not forthcoming, and I lost the cream of my American staff with less than two weeks' advance notice. This included civil affairs officers working alone in isolated villages and senior staff officers with two or more solid years of experience in the Italian, or European, way of doing some things and looking at others. Filling their places required my full attention for more than a month. Eventually the replacements came—virtually all of them from combat units, with no military government experience. Nevertheless, for the most part they were good men; and in a shorter time than I had anticipated, the ordinary business of administration passed the crisis point and settled down.

Another matter that had been slow getting off the ground and required preferred attention at this time was the program for dealing with persons who had perpetrated fascist crimes at any time or collaborated with the Germans after the date of the Italian capitulation and armistice.

The program had two aspects, one criminal in concept: defascism; the other civil or administrative: epuration.

Defascism was the business of the Special Courts of Assize created under the authority of Field Marshal Alexander's Proclamation No. 5, which had been published in June before my arrival. By its terms, it self-destructed six months after publication but this term was extended by subsequent proclamations until March 31, 1947, when an unfinished caseload of 32 minor cases was turned over to the regular Court of Assize. The personnel of the court included five local civilians—a magistrate selected by the first president of the Court of Appeals of Trieste, and four lay assessors selected by the local chief civilian judge from a list of local residents certified by an AMG-appointed committee of local civilians to be of "accepted moral and political probity." A right of appeal to the local Court of Appeals was provided, and death sentences could be carried out only after confirmation in writing by the theater commander or a person deputized by him for the purpose.

During the period of the court's existence, there were 1,269 trials, resulting in 342 convictions and 927 acquittals. The court imposed one death sentence (reduced on appeal), 10 sentences of 30 years' imprisonment, and 257 sentences ranging from 30 months to 30 years.

As might be expected, the local press covered the proceedings very thoroughly, and there was considerable criticism from both sides, usually charging either too much leniency or failure to convict. Most of the complaints were either straight propaganda or reflected a failure to comprehend the requirements of due process, which sometimes resulted in acquittals of persons who might, indeed, have been guilty. This is a condition prevalent in all courts where the rule of law and presumption of innocence prevail.

The epuration program was based on General Order No. 7, which I had signed and published on July 11, 1945, just a week after my arrival in Trieste. As the name suggests, its primary objective was not punishment, but to purify the civil service and some nongovernmental entities affected with the public interest of fascist and collaborationist elements.

In this case, the process was conducted not by a court but by a commission appointed by the area commissioners of each of the three areas and consisting of "citizens of integrity and nonfascist antecedents."

All the employees to whom the epuration process applied were divided by General Order No. 7 into immediate, routine, and postponed categories. Each person within the first two categories was required to fill out and submit to the appropriate commission within fourteen days a *scheda personale*, or questionnaire, covering the relevant circumstances of his or her working, social, and political life to date. The epuration commissions made their decisions on the basis of these questionnaires, augmented by any other evidence they saw fit to adduce from any source.

The action of the commissions consisted of an order either confirming the subject's right to continued employment, or his or her dismissal or suspension. Dismissals and suspensions were subject to appeal to a Territorial Commission of Appeal, and persons suspended or dismissed also had the right to apply to the original local commission for reinstatement if the commission became convinced of their rehabilitation.

On August 20, 1945, I had issued another general order (No. 7A) bringing the postponed category into the epuration process. The trial commissions got down to business at about the same time. By October 1, 298 accused fascists had received notice of proposed suspension, and 9 had been finally dismissed.

A typical case involved Dr. Giancarlo Avvogadro of Gorizia, who had held many honorary fascist titles and had been a participant in the original march on Rome. Evidence on the positive side, however, showed that he was an excellent physician and had given medical aid when required to all who applied, including antifascist partisans. The commission suspended him for a period of eight months from his position as director of the Gorizia Tuberculosis Hospital.

Other items of interest that occurred while we awaited the arrival of the foreign ministers' deputies included, as reflected in my diary:

> *September 24*: A general industrial strike, joined in by both the communist Sindacati Unici and the Italian Sindacati Giuliani, collapsed after one day when the Sindacati Giuliani concluded that Unici was interested more in the political, than in the economic, aspects of labor's claims.
>
> *October 8*: My mother wrote, "The war is over, and if an American must be in that spot (which I do not believe) it should not be the father of four children."
>
> *October 10*: The 88th American Infantry Division, "First In Rome," arrived as part of the permanent garrison, sup-

plementing a British division and corps troops to constitute the custodial force under the command of Lieutenant General Harding. The Blue Devils were a welcome sight to Americans for so long so greatly outnumbered.

October 12: In Bologna by courtesy of Mayor Dozza. I became an honorary citizen of that city at a gala ceremony.

October 13: First turn-out parade and inspection of the Venezia Giulia Police Force; 700 men in the "cerini" uniform.

November 17: We were visited by Field Marshal Alexander, the supreme allied commander, who attended our regular staff meeting and had some very kind words to say about our performance.

November 18–23: I visited Austria, including Vienna, observing AMG methods and procedures, which were very different from ours.

November 25: I presided at ceremonies reopening the University of Trieste; made a faux pas by referring to it as the fifth *Italian* University at whose opening I had assisted; no harm done.

January 11: Lt. Gen. John C. H. ("Court House") Lee, the new American Mediterranean theater commander, visited the area, interviewed me at length, and asked me if I would like to stay to finish the job "I had so far done so well." Heady stuff! I said "yes."

January 19: I was notified that I would be granted a month's home leave before returning to Trieste to finish the job, my deputy, Colonel Robertson (British) to act for me in my absence.

The date of the previous entry was also the day one of the most sensational rumors of the occupation burst upon us: that the USSR would support Italy's claim to Trieste. Even discounting such a possibility, the idea of spending a month or more far away from my job at this particular time suggested some problems.

Naturally, I wanted to go, but had some doubts that the corps commander would agree to my departure, in view of the long-heralded, and now at last apparently imminent, arrival of the commission of foreign ministers' deputies who were to consider a solution to the problem of the permanent boundary, which had been my daily concern for the preceding seven months.

I was wrong. General Harding insisted that I go and even found some tactical public relations advantage in the fact that if I were six thousand miles away I could not be accused of trying to influence the delegates' decision.

I left Italy on February 17 and, as it turned out, did not return to Trieste for more than two months due to unexpected consultations in Washington, both going and coming, with Gen. Arch Hamblen and others, and rather primitive transport arrangements. As it turned out, according to my deputy's report on my return, none of the foreign ministers' deputies arrived until March 7, two days after Mr. Churchill's pointed, specific reference to Trieste in his Iron Curtain speech at Fulton, Missouri. The USSR's delegate, Mr. Gerashcenko, did not show up until March 8. In any event, none of the deputies showed any disposition upon arrival to seek immediate advice or information from the Allied Military Government.

My account of the events of the following sixty days is based on Colonel Robertson's reports and diaries, accounts of other officers, and press reports covering the period.

The arrival of the delegates, of course, was the signal for some of the most ambitious demonstrations of the occupation. Both sides were very active, the object in each case being to demonstrate the overwhelmingly Italian or Slovene/Croat ethnic character of the place of the demonstrations or displays. The predominantly Italian centers of Trieste and Gorizia were adorned with thousands of Italian flags, some bearing the superimposed red star, while the outlying areas and Isonzo Valley Slovene communities responded with more and better Yugoslav flags and triumphal arches, topped with portraits of Tito and a variety of slogans.

A recent order making it a punishable offense to deface public buildings with political graffiti backfired under these conditions. The communist perpetrators of this minor form of sabotage rose to the challenge and actually doubled and redoubled the incidence of political graffiti, and consequently so did the number of arrests for the offense. This in turn provided excuse for the Slovene press and the Belgrade radio to put out desperate stories of persecution and brutality by the "Fascist Venezia Giulia Police under the benevolent protection of AMG."

Parenthetically, the police force was rounding into shape by this time. As a matter of statistics, its ethnic composition was about one Slovene or Croat for every two Italians, and there was no sign of internal dissension attributable to ethnic or political distinctions. The force had made great progress in crowd-control techniques and was used for this purpose, although as a matter of AMG policy this work was done by military police and specially trained Allied troops so far as possible.

It follows that one of the most painful moments during my leave in California came when I read in the *Los Angeles Times* that the police had actually fired on a hostile crowd in Servola, a Trieste suburb, killing two people and wounding eighteen. As I guessed from seven thousand miles' distance, this was just what the Communists wanted and was the occasion for a new outbreak of demonstrations. Several members of the police force were charged with manslaughter, but all were acquitted several months later after an exhaustive public military trial by non-AMG officers. Still, I told myself, the incident would not have happened if I had been on the job. Now, I wonder.

Other than in this special case, the main foci of the demonstrations were the buildings where the Boundary Commission (the foreign ministers' deputies) or any of its members were reported to be present or doing business. The pro-Yugoslav demonstrators, their inferior numbers in Trieste supplemented by hundreds of poor, harried Slovene country people who had tramped all night in order to demonstrate all the following day, initiated the demonstrations outside the target building. Then the pro-Italian demonstrators concentrated on dispersing them. The essential task of the police was to keep the two forces separated as much as possible. To the credit of both the military and the civilian elements, they largely succeeded, and despite the huge, hysterical crowds involved, serious casualties were very few.

On March 26, Tito threw oil on the flames by declaring that he would "resist with full energy" any findings of the Boundary Commission unfavorable to Yugoslavia. This statement, subject to a vast range of interpretations depending on the scope of the word "resist," triggered the largest pro-Italian demonstration since June of the preceding year, when the Yugoslavs had departed. Troop movements noted by military intelligence along the Morgan Line were described by Yugoslav officials as purely defensive, although the only other troops in sight were those of their British and American allies.

Following the departure of the commission in early April and my return mid-month, rumors concerning these troop movements burgeoned. I can have little doubt that these rumors were supported to some extent by further intelligence, if only because they were obviously taken seriously by our corps commander, General Harding. I had little to do with this situation and have no idea to this moment on what information the action he took was based. In any event, at the time—the last half of April—I was preoccupied in trying to catch up with the events that had taken place during my absence.

I also had some important visitors to entertain and inform, and they were all due on the same day. One was Harold Macmillan, who had been His Majesty's resident minister in this part of the world throughout the war, as well as president of the Allied Commission. It was almost eleven years before he was to become prime minister, but his report to the government as a member of parliament could have considerable impact on our credibility and fortunes. The other visitors were a group of America's most powerful publishers, including those of *Time, Life, Fortune, Newsweek,* the *Saturday Evening Post,* the *New York Times,* and many potent and highly influential metropolitan daily newspapers. I showed them the area and was surprised along the way to note a heavy predominance of Italian flags and pennants, with no apparent effort by the Yugoslavs to compete. Could it be that they were considering another course of action? There were those in the military establishment who thought so, and after I had satisfactorily informed Mr. Macmillan and the publishers and responded to their questions, I took measures to inform myself.

To this day, I have never seen any of the intelligence reports that gave rise to the apprehension—a moral certainty on the part of some intelligence officers—that Tito planned to take advantage of May Day/Communist Labor Day euphoria to accomplish a coup d'etat by marching his troops down into Trieste from those hills where they had been encamped. To add to the likelihood of such action, May 1 would be the first anniversary of the takeover of Trieste by Tito's Partisan soldiers.

Prelude to Decision 109

On the other hand, May 2 was also an anniversary of some significance in that part of the world. Locally, it was the day on which the New Zealanders had entered the city and shelled the remaining German troops out of their redoubt in the Palace of Justice. But on a larger scale, it was also the effective date of the document that constituted the final surrender of the Germans in Italy. So what could be more natural than that the Yugoslav Army's allies, the British and Americans, would feel strongly impelled to hold a parade on that day?

Obviously, if a parade were to be held on May 2, the troops participating in it would have to come into the city to prepare for it on May 1. Of course that was May Day, a traditional time for local celebration, but that could not be helped. May Day celebrations within reason need not be canceled, although none of them must be permitted to get in the way of the parade route or the assembly points for it. It may sound like a phony ploy to the cynical, but the logic was sound.

And so it was done. The troops started marching in early on May 1. There were no untoward disturbances, and Tito did not come down from the hills or send any of his men. The British and American troops preempted all the favorite demonstration places, and the parade the following day, reviewed by the corps and theater commanders, was a thrilling sight to behold.

Four days after the parade, the British Broadcasting Company reported on the morning news that the USSR had proposed that Trieste and its environs be awarded to Yugoslavia in return for certain concessions to Italy in the way of restoration of colonies, diminished reparations, and the like. Mr. Bevin, the Labour foreign minister of Great Britain, replied that Great Britain would not in this manner traffic in human lives; the wishes of the people must be considered first of all. This in turn raised the specter of a possible plebiscite, for which we certainly were not prepared. More attention to the preparation of complete and up-to-date electoral rolls was clearly indicated. For historical reasons, they would not constitute a completely satisfactory plebiscite enrollment, but at least we would have done what we could.

As was later disclosed, but is not really a part of my story, no consensus was ever reached by or between any two of the foreign ministers' deputies constituting the recently departed Boundary

Commission. The line proposed by the USSR conformed almost exactly to Tito's most extravagant claim. The French representative proposed a line not differing greatly from the Austria-Italy border of the days before the First World War; the Americans and British agreed, except that they tried to give Italy a little more land than did the French representative.

The Council of Foreign Ministers reviewed the reports and heard the arguments of the foreign ministers of Italy and Yugoslavia. By the end of their first session, about mid-May, it had become apparent that the French position was most favored. They reconvened in mid-June, and on July 3 announced the solution they would propose to the peace conference. Italy would cede to Yugoslavia all territory east of the line proposed by the French. Land west of that line would remain Italian from the Austrian border to the Adriatic near Monfalcone. The area south of Duino and west of the French line would form an independent Free Territory of Trieste, whose governor would be appointed; its security and independence would be guaranteed by the Security Council of the United Nations.

It is beyond the scope of this memoir to speculate about the reasons for the decision. It may have represented what the foreign ministers' deputies who constituted the boundary commission reported to their chiefs as the consensus of the people who had been dealing with the problem on the ground during the preceding year. On the other hand, it is equally likely that it was simply a typical Great Powers compromise. To the USSR it might have seemed that giving the city and its port to Italy would lead to the exclusive use of the port by the Western bloc. On the other hand, as things stood at that time, to assign them to Yugoslavia might have seemed to the Western powers likely to bring them under the domination of the forces behind the Iron Curtain. Creation of an international territory would leave the city and port open to both East and West.

In retrospect, one may speculate that the Soviet motives in this matter were similar to those that I have suggested might have had something to do with the relatively smooth process of disarming the partisans in Emilia two years earlier. Stalin's only alternative, as he saw it, might have been to start a new war with his late allies, and he was too deeply involved in other projects to consider such action.

The United Nations Organization, or UNO as it was called in those days, had enjoyed its finest hour. The United States had confirmed the U.N. Charter just a year earlier and on the preceding October 24, when the final ratifications had been deposited by the Ukrainian and Byelorussian Soviet Socialist Republics, the Charter, in the words of U.S. Secretary of State Edward Stettinius two days later, had become "a part of the law of nations." At this point optimism and euphoria still reigned concerning the United Nations' potential to maintain peace forever.

It was therefore, perhaps, only natural that it should occur to the harried delegates to the peace conference that the special problems of Trieste might best be solved within the framework of the new world organization of states. One can reasonably argue that it was as a result of this kind of unselfish world-minded thinking that the first world state, the Free Territory of Trieste, was born.

Certainly, the idealistic, optimistic international political liberals of the Western world were sincerely ecstatic about the idea. And for good reason. "UNO's first-born!" Would there be other offspring? What might not the possibilities be for similar handling of other trouble spots should this experiment succeed? Could it be hoped that, working together of necessity on the small day-to-day problems of the Little Mouse State (so dubbed by Italian satirists), member-nations of the Security Council might gradually learn to work together similarly in larger affairs? The most euphoric foresaw in prospect the utopian time of Tennyson's prophecy, when

> . . . the war drums throbbed no longer
> and the battle flags were furled
> In the Parliament of Man,
> the federation of the World.

Whatever the thinking at higher levels, the reaction locally was violent. It had become known, as such things always are, that the British and American views presented to both the Boundary Commission and the foreign ministers had been much more favorable to the Italians than the eventual decision, and the feeling that Uncle Sam and John Bull would win out in the end had lulled the locals into what turned out to be a false euphoria. The letdown produced some of the roughest times we ever faced. For the first time, even British and American troops (particularly the former) were attacked, and the city had to be declared off limits or, as the British called it, "out of bounds."

At this sensitive time, trouble broke out over a bicycle race. I shall never know whether or not it was intended as a deliberate provocation, but certainly if I had been consulted I would have protested the extension into the zone of any race or contest billed as All-Italy, as this bicycle race was. This was a natural target for Yugoslav disruption. Of course, the intrusion of anything labeled All-Italy would have been a provocation at any time. This particular outbreak occurred at Pieris, on May 30, when pro-Yugoslav saboteurs and provocateurs rolled barrels and strewed nails in the bicyclists' path. When the police attempted to disperse the attackers, they were fired upon, and one policeman was wounded.

Since the *Giro d'Italia* was a sporting event dear to all Italians, the indignation of the local ones when they heard what had happened was immense. Bands of youths roamed the streets smashing Slovene shop windows and communist clubs. That day's edition of *Il Lavoratore*, the communist-oriented newspaper, was set ablaze, but promptly reprinted and distributed by the Allied Information Service. The Slovene bookshop, where my poor calumniated alleged Slovene mistress was employed, was sacked.

In the midst of all this, my personal assistant, Junior Commander Elizabeth Penrith, attempted to get to the beach in one of my cars driven by the normally imperturbable Alfredo. Her companion was Rosemary Anderson, assistant to William Sullivan, the local British political adviser and later British ambasssador to Mexico. They were required to force their way through a particularly nasty portion of the turmoil. Elizabeth, frightened, admits to have cowered, and even Alfredo was scared to death. Not Rosemary, as Elizabeth recently recalled. "Sit up straight, Elizabeth," she said sharply. "Remember you are British." Elizabeth managed somehow to remain erect. Actually, they don't come more British than the then Miss Penrith.

The local press published highly colored versions of the previous day's rioting, claiming that the police had favored the pro-Italian rioters, and the communist-oriented labor union called a general strike that lasted twelve days.

Both sides were indignant and dissatisfied with the proposed solution to the boundary question. Tito declared he would never give up Yugoslav claims to Trieste, Gorizia, or the Slovene littoral. The Italians were particularly bitter about the loss of the Istrian peninsula, especially its west coast where there was no doubt the population was overwhelmingly composed of ethnic Italians, most of whom it was said would leave rather than submit to rule by the "Schiavi." The proposed free state was referred to by both sides as a "midget abortion" and the Italian press labeled it "Topolino" or "Little Mouse," fancying to find in its contours on the map the shape of a small rodent whose body reclined curled around the upper end of the Adriatic. The Italians continued to hope and push for a plebiscite—if not at once, then perhaps in five years.

Such was the unenviable situation we faced in British–American-occupied Venezia Giulia on the eve of the peace conference scheduled to begin on July 29. Fuel was added to the flames by a story in the *Washington Times-Herald* just two days before that date, under the head: "Was Trieste Promised to Stalin?," based on Henry J. Taylor's just-published book, *Men and Power*. I quote in part from the newspaper article:

> According to Mr. Taylor, Stalin as early as the beginning of 1942, had set his heart on getting the Persian Gulf port of Basra as one of Russia's war prizes, and had spoken of this aim in no uncertain terms to Anthony Eden and Cordell Hull.
>
> At the Teheran conference in late 1943, the story goes on, Winston Churchill was all ready with a counter-offer to Stalin. Churchill's government, of course, wanted if possible to keep Russia off the Persian Gulf, which overlooks the British Empire route to India. So Churchill is asserted to have offered Trieste to Stalin after the war if Stalin would forget about Basra.
>
> Roosevelt, who was also at the Teheran Conference, evidently sat by and consented to all this. According to this report, Stalin was overjoyed at the prospect of moving Russian influence to the top of the Adriatic.
>
> The story sounds reasonable, Certainly Russia now controls Rumania, Hungary, and Yugoslavia, and our present-day Allied statesmen have made no vigorous moves to break up that control. And certainly Marshal Tito, Stalin's puppet pro-consul of Yugoslavia, acts as if he thought he had legal title to Trieste.

Obviously, this kind of story was not what we needed at that moment in history!

The Home Stretch

British and American tanks passing in review, May 2, 1946

Following the collapse of the twelve-day general strike in mid-July, things quieted down a bit, but I had to cope almost at once with an extremely irritating incident of a totally different character. It was rumored that Fiorello La Guardia, former mayor of New York and now director general of the United Nations Relief and Rehabilitation Administration (UNRRA), was in the neighborhood. A bit later in the month, Maj. Gen. Bryant Moore, commanding general of the U.S. 88th Division, phoned me at my villa in the evening.

"The Little Flower is coming in tomorrow," he said, "and I'd be grateful if you'd take care of him. Can you supply a convoy to meet him at the Udine airport tomorrow?"

I enjoyed an especially friendly relationship with General Moore, who occupied an anomalous position in the local channels of command, and one that made me particularly vulnerable. Operationally, I was a staff officer of the British 13th Corps, commanded by General Harding, but for administrative purposes I had to belong to an American unit, which in this case was the Military Government Detachment of the 88th Division. Among other things, this meant that General Moore prepared my efficiency report, although he exercised no command over me and had nothing whatever directly to do with military government per se. He could have resented that fact, to the detriment of my military record.

Fortunately, General Harding and General Moore had taken to each other immediately, and since General Harding always evinced very high regard for my abilities and performance, I did not suffer. In fact, I never enjoyed better efficiency reports during my service. Nevertheless, I was always glad of an opportunity to do a favor for the commanding general, 88th Division, who in the years ahead became a close personal friend before he lost his life in Korea while on his way to a corps command there. So I readily undertook the task of looking after Mr. La Guardia.

Not only on the next day, but on the two days following, the AMG fleet of Alfa Romeos and my own personal Buick proceeded to the airport in charge of a senior American officer and waited all day for the Great Man to arrive. Nothing happened at the airport, but something did at Belgrade where Mr. La Guardia, somehow, had arrived without stopping at Trieste. There were shortages in shipments of UNRRA goods destined for Yugoslavia, he announced to the world press assembled in the Yugoslav capital, and they were all due to nonfeasance or malfeasance by the Allied Military Government at Trieste, the point of entry.

How did the little man know this? Apparently Tito told him, because there was certainly never any investigation in Trieste. There had been thefts at the docks, but they were inconsiderable. I had foreseen the possibility of such claims months before and had adopted stringent measures to prevent any irregularities. The skirts of the police were completely clean.

There can be no doubt that any shortfall in the delivery of UNRRA and other supplies to Yugoslavia during the summer of 1946 was due primarily, if not exclusively, to the general strikes that characterized this period. These were critical indeed, at times requiring the use as stevedores of personnel of the Royal (British) Engineers and of German prisoners of war. Since the general strike was mainly caused by propaganda and covert instructions to the dockworkers emanating directly from the source of the complaints expressed to Mr. La Guardia in Belgrade, his diatribe seemed to us, to put it mildly, a bit unfair.

Within 24 hours after the Little Flower's outburst, a dozen officers arrived from Allied Force Headquarters, investigated the entire situation, and satisfied themselves that there was no merit in the accusations. The theater commander sent a stinging reply to Mr. La Guardia, ending with an invitation for him to come to Trieste and observe and investigate the situation himself. He never did, and my admiration for the Little Flower was somewhat abated.

The press correspondents on hand at the time—many of them specifically for the purpose of reporting Mr. La Guardia's visit—told me that this sort of thing was nothing new, that trial without evidence and condemnation without a hearing was one of Mr. La Guardia's favorite pastimes. "Strictly a phony," said one reporter. "Completely honest, but that's all," said another. I would not accept these evaluations, but Mr. La Guardia was certainly totally wrong, unfair, and intemperate this time.

The only occasion on which we may have felt more let down by a distinguished visitor was when Gen. Dwight D. Eisenhower came to see us the following month and didn't even leave the Udine airport.

While Mr. La Guardia's bad manners and ready acceptance of our adversary's evaluation of our performance hurt our pride and, to a degree, diminished our respect for him as a public figure, it did not affect his popularity with the people of Venezia Giulia, or in Italy generally. Known to be a very important American politician of Italian descent, he continued to enjoy great prestige.

Less than three months after his promised but aborted visitation, it had become clear that the treaty of peace with Italy was almost certain to create a free territory surrounding the city, to be administered by a governor appointed by the Security Council of the United Nations. When, thereupon, the university newspaper *Caleidoscopio* conducted a local survey addressed to the question: "What personality in all the world would you desire as governor of the future free state of Trieste?," the Little Flower led by a considerable margin.

It was, by the way, a matter of some satisfaction to "Bowman Infamoso," the daily target of the most awful accusations in the same publication as well as its opposition press, that the people's second choice was Col. Alfred C. Bowman of Los Angeles; third choice was Field Marshal Alexander; fourth was Msgr. Antonio Santin, the Roman Catholic bishop of Trieste. Very worthy company.

Bearing in mind that it would still be a long time before one could even be sure that there would ever be a free territory, the speculation and parade of candidates in the press in the months following the *Caleidoscopio* poll were fascinating exercises. On November 29, 1946, James Reston published a "want ad" column in the *New York Times* outlining necessary qualifications and specifications for the job. The headline read: "Man Wanted for Trieste Job; Must Be Young and Brave." The subhead was more explicit: "Exciting Future Assured for Able Diplomat, Linguist, Financier and Traffic Expert." Reston predicted that the future governor of Trieste "would be the keeper of the fate of Central Europe."

This job description could not displease the colonel who had been actually handling most aspects of the position for a year and a half, but there was more to come. In an editorial in the respectable *Richmond Times-Dispatch*, publisher Virginius Dabney, a great newspaperman, actually nominated me informally for the permanent U. N. job. Could this actually happen? Was it a viable or desirable possibility? I asked Sir John Harding what he thought.

I have never been more continuously confident of the approbation of a superior over an extended period of time than I was of Sir John's. "No, Al," he said, "I'd forget it if I were you. You're too compromised. I don't mean that in any derogatory sense. What I do mean is that by virtue of your job you are identified with a policy and point of view that are not by any means universally shared in the world community. This is a job for a politician, a man like Robert Murphy or Harold Macmillan."

I relinquished my momentary dream without too much pain, remembering some of Scotty Reston's specifications. But again I was pleased by the company in which I found myself.

Actually, most of the candidates for governor nominated by the major powers during the ensuing months and years were politicians—usually retired or retiring ministers of the smaller and less involved nations, like Switzerland, Sweden, Belgium, and the less important Soviet bloc countries. The treaty that created the Free Territory of Trieste provided that the new state would come into existence upon the appointment and arrival in Trieste of the governor. So the naming of one of the candidates would have triggered the mechanism that would have made the first world state a reality. Perhaps for this reason, no one was appointed during the ensuing 28 years. Whether this is cause for sorrow or rejoicing is a subject for individual evaluation. Some reflections on it will appear later.

Considering the apparently great preponderance of local sentiment on both the pro-Italian and pro-Yugoslav sides against the solution that was now actually proposed by the foreign ministers, it took considerable courage for a small political group who actually favored such a solution, to say so. Such a group was the Fronte dell' Indipendenza. Not unnaturally, they now began to come forward. Having come closer than anyone else to espousing from the beginning the solution now proposed, they felt the time might be appropriate for them to take over all, or at least a major part, of the existing governmental structure.

With the greatest of admiration for their courage in having promoted at an early stage an unpopular solution in which it now appeared likely the world's major governments would concur, I told them that until the treaty was signed and became effective, I felt it my duty to maintain the status quo as far as possible. "There's many a slip 'twixt the cup and the lip," and all that. Be patient, I advised. They conformed, but I'm sure their patience must have been severely tried during the years that lay ahead.

I have been informed on a confidential basis by a considerable number of Triestini and Americans of Triestini descent, that during those years the secret sentiment in favor of the solution proposed by the foreign ministers was much stronger and more widespread than could be guessed from any personal expressions or objective evidence. The people who felt that way, I have been told time after time, were simply too frightened in the face of the threatened violence from both of the all-or-nothing sides, to express their views.

The summer of 1946 was an important and sometimes critical time in another respect, which had nothing to do with local politics: American families began to arrive. This should have been good news all around, but such was not always the case. Many of the men, including officers, had now been totally separated from their families for four years or more and in a relatively exotic, though war-torn, foreign community for the past three. Personal associations, including some involving deep personal attachment, had been formed. These had to be broken or the family destroyed. It wasn't easy, and there were many small tragedies.

In the special case of Trieste, and in my own very special case as the head of a highly controversial government, it seemed advisable for reasons of personal security and safety not to bring all the American families directly into the city. For the families of some senior officers, including military government personnel, a special community was established on the Venice Lido—the long hotel-laden sandbar that forms a natural breakwater between the open Adriatic and the lagoon of Venice. There my family and others, thought to be in special danger by reason of the position of the family head, were maintained in fine villas with servants and other amenities. I became a weekend commuter when operational requirements permitted, flying to the Lido by light aircraft on Fridays or Saturdays and returning Sundays. It was not a wholly satisfactory arrangement within which to renew a family relationship that had been interrupted for almost four years, but it had to do, and most of us lived through it without permanent scars.

In the case of many of the junior people, who were not regarded as so controversial as to make their dependents likely targets for violence or kidnapping, living quarters were found in or near Trieste, aggravating the housing shortage and subjecting military government to even more local criticism. On the other hand, it was always something of a relief to the local landlord to have his property requisitioned and rented by an American or British family, and this sentiment tended to offset the annoyance of having the places requisitioned at all.

When the American families arrived, many British families were already in place, their government having acted more expeditiously and the logistical problems being much less—merely a matter of getting on a train in London and getting off at Trieste.

The British operation, by the way, was always described as relating to married families. The Americans were amused by this redundance. "What other kind of families are there?" they asked. Sometimes, in a moment of candor, a pukka poona wallah who had served in India would tell a puzzled American about another kind of family with which the British armed services had had to cope in the great days of Empire. It became clear that the word "married," against this background, was not redundant.

When the peace conference convened in late July, determination of the fate of Venezia Giulia still awaited the formulation of the treaty, its signing by the delegates to the conference from each of the forty-odd nations involved, and finally ratification by the signatory nations by whatever means their constitutions or traditions required. As it turned out, ratification by France and the USSR was not to take place until June 1947.

Nevertheless, there can be no doubt that locally we all began to feel that the pressure was off, that "it was all over but the shouting," although certainly a lot of shouting lay ahead. The presence of families contributed to the realization that, even for military government personnel in embattled Venezia Giulia, the war was really over. Officers who had come to feel that the jobs they were doing might well become their permanent careers, looked at their wives and children and realized that, after all, their futures probably lay in the continental United States. The social side of life began to loom more prominently. Tempers cooled a bit in the community.

One serious operational problem still to be confronted was the anticipated massive exodus of Italians from the Italian town (and former Italian naval base) at Pola. Nothing could be done to stem the departure of these people, nor would anyone on either side have wished to do so. This was a matter for personal and family decision, and many thousands did indeed opt to leave and take their chances on a livelihood, or charity at the hands of their compatriots, on the Italian "mainland."

The exodus from Pola by a considerable part of the Italian population commenced officially on December 27, 1946, and was completed by March 31, 1947, although there can be no doubt that many thousands who chose not to participate in the official program left sooner, and many afterwards, using their own means.

In any event, 2,500 families participated in a program that had the official support of the Italian government and the assistance of the Italian Red Cross. The household goods of these families were transported to Trieste by motorships, small motor- and sailing-craft traveling in convoy, and by rail. In Trieste, the household goods were stored in warehouses of the Magazzino Generale at the Duke of Aosta port, arranged in such fashion that articles could be withdrawn, upon showing of a receipt, as they were needed or as means could be found to forward them to a destination in Italy proper.

Unfortunately, there were some problems. A considerable segment of Pola's economy was disrupted by the removal of such objects as tools and machinery from workshops, furniture from inns and restaurants, and pharmacists' equipment. A special and pervasive problem involved efforts to dismantle and take away industrial plants whose continued operation was vital to the survival of the portion of Pola's population that chose not to leave. A case in point was a flour mill. That dispute reached the ambassadorial level and required the personal attention of the theater commander. I believe that eventually the plant stayed in Pola, and a way was found to compensate its departing owners.

Another serious civil affairs problem we encountered during the winding down period was a shortage of cemetery space. You don't have to dig deep anywhere in Venezia Giulia to hit limestone, which is sufficiently impermeable to make it unfit for burials. For centuries the custom in this part of the world had been to bury the bodies for a dozen years or so, until they disintegrated into a heap of bones that could be interred in a very small space, either in the ground or in a cemetery wall similar to those used for cremated remains in American commercial mausoleums. Since even space for temporary burial was running out in the vicinity of Trieste, in early 1947 we undertook, as a public works project, the construction of a ten-body-deep underground mausoleum—the first in which the bodies of paupers would enjoy equal rights with those of the rich.

Nevertheless, the trend during the fall, winter, and spring months was away from new projects. The realization grew that it was time to start giving more attention to recording what we had done. I put two officers to work full time on two histories of our operation—one organized by function and the other arranged chronologically. In early December, the word came from higher authority: "Start to wind up."

This was also a period of many visitors. More publishers from back home came and went by the planeload. In early December, as the senior American on the corps staff, I chatted with Field Marshal Bernard Law Montgomery at dinner at the corps mess, finding him a much smaller man than he had seemed in those early pictures from Alamein and looking very school teacherish in mufti. Writer Alan Moorhead stayed for some time. General Lee, the theater commander, came often. On one occasion, he embarrassed us and caused massive incredulity in the civilian community by calling publicly for an AMG campaign to stamp out prostitution in a central European city where it had been a recognized, if not an honored, profession since the dawn of history.

Then there was Christmas and everything that went with the season. One of these events—peculiar to Venezia Giulia as far as I know—was the fish harvest at Monfalcone. Once a year, by custom since time immemorial, and possibly with some ecological justification, the fishermen were permitted to enclose a portion of the lagoon with a monstrous net and to sweep in literally every fish in the net's path. Not without misgivings, I helped them on December 4.

Also in accordance with ancient custom, as the substitute for ancient emperors and dukes I found myself deluged with the kind of letters from children that at home would be addressed only to Santa Claus, and later I was required to play the Saint Nicholas part in Christmas parties at schools and orphanages and at the opening of a communal kitchen. The day after Christmas, I was the guest and roastee at a Bell for Bowman party given by our enlisted men. The allusion was to John Hersey's then recently published novel, *A Bell for Adano*, whose plot was soon to be duplicated locally in Barbana.

Barbana is a small island in the Gulf of Venice near the eastern border of my AMG domain, about a mile offshore from the resort and fishing village of Grado, to which it then belonged for AMG administrative purposes. On it stands the three-centuries-old church and monastery, La Madonna di Barbana. Its inhabitants in

1946 were twenty Franciscan friars. For a hundred years, they told the military government officer in Grado, they had been praying for a bell that would be loud enough to be heard on the mainland, giving comfort to its people.

Two years earlier, John Hersey's book had dealt with a similar problem in Sicily, which was solved by the creation of a new bell from the metal in guns left behind by the Germans. As had happened in Grado, the Germans had left behind a battery of guns that were at one time intended to guard the Gulf of Trieste from Allied invaders.

Charles Molfetto, the American officer in charge of AMG business in Grado, was a man of action. After taking the matter up with me, he set about doing what had to be done. There was enough metal not only to make the big bell the monks and people wanted, but also to replace the smaller bells already in the church, which were virtually worn out. I journeyed to the island for the dedication on a cold, damp winter day with a number of my colleagues who had participated in the operation.

"It is fitting," I told the friars, "that here in Grado, far from the Sicilian scene portrayed in *A Bell for Adano*—a work immortalizing the early days of AMG in Italy—the closing acts of that same military government should include today a presentation to the people of this other extreme outpost of Italy of a Bell for Barbana."

A few months later, two of the friars visited me in my office in Trieste, to present me with three small replicas of the big bell; one for myself, one for the pope, and one for the president of the United States. Not having immediate personal access to either of the latter persons, I asked Bishop Santin of Trieste to deliver the bell earmarked for Pius XII and enlisted Bill Cole, the local American political advisor, to deliver the third one to President Truman. Neither of the recipients, I'm sorry to say, ever acknowledged receipt.

Another type of ceremony, always pleasant and sometimes highly enjoyable, involved presenting to their owners the keys to, and physical possession of, their homes—usually in the smaller villages, which had been destroyed by the Germans and rebuilt for them by us.

A typical occasion of this kind was the rebirth of the town of

Bretto di Sopra, well up on the south slope of the Alps, north of Gorizia. The Christmas Day issue of the 88th Division's newspaper, the *Blue Devil*, reported:

> In a ceremony held Sunday 22 December at Bretto di Sopra, new homes were presented to the people by Colonel Alfred C. Bowman . . . of AMG. These homes were rebuilt by AMG at no cost to the people, following their destruction during the war.
>
> As part of the program, a film was shown to the people of the village and the guests, showing the village as it was before the reconstruction work was started, and the different stages of development of the work until it was finished. The group then removed to the (town) square where the blessing, and a short speech, were delivered by the priest of Plezzo. He thanked AMG on behalf of the villagers, and stated that this would be a great Christmas for them, as they could now return to their homes for the first time in three years. Following this, Colonel Bowman made a speech, before handing out the keys to the houses to the people, in which he stated that although AMG would soon be leaving the area, it was glad to be of help to the people in rebuilding their villages as long as it is here. The American Red Cross was present to give out toys to the children and coffee to everyone. A few of the houses were inspected before a luncheon was given for the visitors.
>
> Bretto di Sopra was classified as a distressed village last August, and work was started on 14 August to rebuild it at a cost to AMG of about 30 million lire. A total of 33 houses were rebuilt in this short time, even though there were a number of difficulties to overcome. The work was entrusted to the contractors Triestina Appalti e Costruzioni (T.A.E.C.) of Trieste, who had to have the mines and bombs put there by the Germans removed by a bomb disposal squad. The work was rushed to have it finished by Christmas.
>
> The village had its start some 200 years ago, when mountain dwellers settled in the area. The development of the village was very slow because of its remote location and it survived the last war without special event until it was completely destroyed on 11 November 1943. On this day, a group of cars carrying German soldiers was fired on as they were passing through the village. Some of the soldiers were killed, and others wounded. The SS Police Guards immediately arrested all the men of the village. The next morning the women and children were taken away and then the men, 16 in number, were dragged behind the houses in the center of the village and shot to death without trial.

Since this reopening took place in mid-winter, the festivities were limited. When the weather got warmer in the following spring and early summer, similar key delivery ceremonies at San Daniele on May 17, Comeno on June 5, Montespino on June 11, and elsewhere, were considerably more festive. I played bocce (the local version of lawn bowling) with the men, was photographed over and over again with both my own children and those of the village, and otherwise tried to accommodate my own demeanor to that of the local citizens—in all respects, that is, short of imbibing the liquor of the towns, which was beyond my tolerance.

The handing-over of the rebuilt villages to their inhabitants was only one of many types of festive ceremonial naturally and appropriately incident to our comprehensive public works program. Throughout the area, hospitals were built or repaired, swamps drained, stumps pulled, soil spread over rocky terrain to make more agricultural land, and tunnels and roads constructed to facilitate the rebirth of commerce. The shipyards at Monfalcone, reactivated under AMG, actually began to turn out finished ships, requiring full-scale ship-launching ceremonies, as early as October 1946. The laying of a cornerstone for a new children's hospital was another such event.

The official justification for these ceremonies, from the viewpoint of the military government, was that they were effective, along with the work itself, in "preventing disease and unrest," one of the basic objectives of our mission.

The prime object of the work itself, at the time and place where it was carried out, was to provide employment, both during the course of reconstruction and in the enterprises to be carried out in the reconstructed facilities. We also thought we could diminish the potential for unrest by providing better living and working conditions. In the case of the villages, a third objective was to encourage the movement back to their hometowns of people who had fled to the metropolis and, while there, were potential fuel for the political passions and disorders that the ideological contenders in Trieste were constantly on the alert to foment.

While the military and strategic justification for the projects whose completion was celebrated on these occasions was officially to house and employ the people and keep them out of mischief, the personal motives of the American and British personnel who participated in the work were not always exclusively operational. We were, in effect, licensed by our nations to play Santa Claus for patriotic reasons and we found the role pleasurable and gratifying. Many of the reconstructed villages were located in Slovene areas now part of Yugoslavia, and even today, I am informed by American friends of Slovene ancestry, residents of the rebuilt towns privately express a high degree of gratitude for the work we did, although in the exercise of discretion and the instinct for self-preservation they would rather not be named or quoted.

In addition to the strictly line-of-duty occasions such as those I have described, there were others of a somewhat less obviously operational nature: a party at the university where the students presented me with one of those tasseled, festooned, long-peaked student hats, which I still cherish; the traditional outdoor Easter Fair on San Giusto Hill, featuring the games and other attractions that characterize spring fairs wherever in the world they are held.

I attended all of these nonoperational affairs unescorted, except when another officer also happened to want to go. Unless someone outside of AMG was doing it for me (without my knowledge) there were none of the elaborate security precautions that are supposed to be required for the personal safety of controversial persons on public occasions involving large crowds of people. This was a source of great concern to some of my security-minded subordinates, and, from their standpoint, rightfully so.

In the light of later events in every part of the world and the excoriation to which I was then being subjected everyday from every direction, it remains a source of grateful wonder to me that through it all, driving my own jeep up and down the hills, or my own horse for miles through great ambush country, I was never threatened with attack, so far as I know. There was, of course, the statement of intent by the friend of Maria Pasquinelli who was to have potted me as she shot Robin de Winton, had I not been absent in Rome—an episode I will describe later. I also remember that at one time my wife told me that a bomb disposal squad had quietly removed several live ones from the terrace of my villa overlooking the city and the harbor. But nothing overt, in the sense in which that word is used to characterize such matters these days, ever took place.

Arrivederci, Bowman

Village girl offers flowers to the author at village reopening ceremony

Nineteen forty-seven was a good year. In the United States, Harry Truman was president, busy with the housing shortage, which he called "the foremost of the many problems facing the nation." The colleges were overflowing with discharged veterans returning to school on the G.I. Bill of Rights. Jackie Robinson signed with the Brooklyn Dodgers to become the first black baseball player in the National League. *Gentlemen's Agreement* won the Academy Award for motion pictures, *A Streetcar Named Desire* was the Broadway hit of the year, and *All the King's Men* won the Pulitzer Prize for literature. People sang "How are Things in Glocca Mora?" from *Finian's Rainbow* and "Almost Like Being in Love" from *Brigadoon*.

Locally, in Venezia Giulia, the first hair-raising event of the year came to pass at a military New Year's Eve party at Miramare Castle not more than five minutes after midnight. Following the usual horn-blowing and kissing, the wife of one of my kilted Scottish officers undertook a violent, freewheeling, one-person demonstration of the Highland Fling. She was a large and athletic woman, and the show was superb, enhanced no end by the fact that the lady was very, very, pregnant and dressed in a manner that in no way concealed that fact. I could not believe that it would be possible to avoid an only-slightly-premature childbirth on the ballroom floor.

As has happened before, I was wrong. Both mother and unborn child survived the performance in good health. Before the end of the month, "it was boy."

Following the holidays, the winding down approach to the job continued to be stressed. The Economic Commission of the Council of Foreign Ministers, whose job it was to be concerned about the commercial and industrial future of both the Free Territory and the contiguous segments of Italy and Yugoslavia that had been excluded from it, arrived on January 6. I testified before the commission later in the month, but its main attention was properly fixed on the civilian leaders of the industrial and commercial community and the appropriate ministers of the contending nations. The fact that the British representative had been an official of the now-defunct Allied Commission for Italy made explanations of why things were done in a certain manner less essential than might otherwise have been the case.

One thing that was not good in Trieste was the weather. However, considering the situation, bad weather was in many ways a good thing. I have elaborated upon this theme elsewhere. Demonstrations and other forms of disorder never persist long in the face of Bora-borne snow, and there was plenty of it. The members of the Economic Commission were impressed with the quietness of the city and wondered aloud where all those stories had come from about the so-called Balkan powder keg.

Another important event in its potential for influence on my personal life, if not on the world, occurred on January 11 in Venice. My family fell in love with and acquired proprietary rights to a French poodle, in Italy called a *Barbino*. They named him Jughaid. No one ever suggested that the first syllable of that name connoted any bias, pro or con, concerning our late allies on the east side of the Morgan Line, nor did either the pro-Italian or pro-Yugoslav factions attempt to find any other political implications in this event. Jughaid was, however, destined to be a Very Important Personality within my family for many years to come.

On the operational side, the foreign ministers, including Yugoslavia's, did at long last sign the Treaty of Peace with Italy, with its Section II and Annexes VI through X designed to create the Free Territory of Trieste and make provision for its control and government. On the same day, the Italian female zealot Maria Pasquinelli assassinated British Brigadier Robin de Winton in Pola. Understanding the nature and significance of this event requires knowing some background concerning the relationship of Pola to the issue of irredentism.

As I indicated in my Introduction, to the north of the city of Trieste from its outskirts to the Austrian border and west to the Isonzo River, most of the geography of the occupied zone was historically Slovene, as were its people. The Istrian peninsula to the south, however, was rimmed by small coastal communities that were predominantly Italian. The most important of these was Pola (now Pula) at the southern tip of the peninsula, which had been developed as a naval base under Austria-Hungary and so used by Italy after 1918. Much of its large Italian population had already migrated to the Italian boot following announcement of the terms of the treaty the preceding November.

Because of its usefulness to Allied naval vessels, Pola, an enclave separated from Trieste by a hundred miles of Yugoslav-administered occupied territory, had been a part of my military government domain from the beginning. It presented no special military government problems, and military government personnel actually stationed there could be counted on the fingers of one hand. However, the British 13th Infantry Brigade was maintained in the town as a security or emergency force. It was commanded by Brigadier R. W. M. (Robin) de Winton, D. S. O., and its headquarters opened upon a main public thoroughfare.

At about 9:30 on the morning of February 10, an automobile in which Brigadier de Winton was the principal passenger drew up just short of the headquarters entrance. The brigadier had alighted and begun to address the five-man Headquarters Guard when a woman in a red coat suddenly appeared about a yard behind him and fired three pistol shots into his back, which killed him almost instantly. Arrested on the spot, the assassin was found to have upon her person a handwritten statement dated the same day, which was translated substantially as follows:

> Pola, 10 February 1947
>
> Following the example of the 600,000 men who fell in the War of Redemption, 1915–18, and feeling as they did the appeal of Oberdan, who add their harassing supplications to those of thousands of Julians whom the Jugoslavs have buried in caves (foibas) from September 1943 to the present day and whose only crime was that of being Italian, at Pola, capital of Istria, wet with the blood of the martyred *Sauro*, I reconfirm the indissolubility of the chain which binds the Motherland to the most Italian lands of Zara, Fiume, and Venezia Giulia, our heroic bastions against the Panslavism which threatens all Western civilization.
>
> I rise in rebellion—firmly determined to strike down in death one who had the misfortune to represent them—against the Big Four who, 'at the conference of Paris, in outrage to any sense of justice, humanity or political wisdom, have decided to wrench once more from the maternal bosom the lands most sacred to Italy, condemning them either to the experience of a new Danzig or—with the most cold consciousness which makes them equally guilty—the Jugoslav yoke, synonym to our indomitably Italian people of death in foibas, of deportation, of exile.
>
> Maria Pasquinelli

Obviously, her note revealed Signorina Pasquinelli to be an obsessed irredentist, as that term has been defined earlier. The War of Redemption must be understood to mean the conflict that we refer to as World War I but which, to the irredentist, was waged solely to redeem the theretofore unredeemed persons and places named by Signorina Pasquinelli and discussed earlier in this book.

By way of further explanation, Guglielmo Oberdan (for whom one of the major piazzas of Trieste is named), was born in Trieste in 1858, but fled to Rome in 1878 to evade the army service required of all Austrian citizens. When he returned to Trieste in 1882 during a celebration of the fifth centennial of Austrian rule, he was tried, found guilty, and executed after being found in possession of two bombs with which, it was charged, he had intended to kill the Emperor Franz Joseph. His death is said to have triggered the activation of the Irredentist Party. Guglielmo Sauro, born in Capodistria in 1880, defected to the Italian navy in 1914 and fought against Austria in the War of Redemption. Following his later capture and trial by the Austrians, he was hanged.

The investigation I called for revealed that Signorina Pasquinelli was a fairly well-known former fascist of the mystical school who had been a school teacher, religiously devoted to Italy and, particularly, to the fascist regime. She had also served as a Red Cross nurse during the war in Africa. There was little doubt as to the sincerity of her sentiments and even less as to her intent and total lack of remorse. The investigation also revealed that she had planned the time, place, and precise symbolic date for the killing of Robin de Winton. Slightly more than a month after the assassination, I ordered that she be tried by a military court, which I directed be convened at the Palace of Justice in Trieste on March 19.

The evidence at the trial fully confirmed the facts as they had been reported to me. The accused's only defense might have been described as that of subjective compulsion or state of necessity (based on Article 54 of the Italian Criminal Code): that her patriotism and the emotional anguish occasioned by the mutilation of Italia Irredenta and its insult to Italian history compelled her, even against her conscious will, to do the act. She was represented by very able counsel, Advocate Luigi Giannini, whose argument to the court was masterful and eloquent. Nevertheless, on April 10, 1947, exactly two months following the date of her act, she was inevitably determined to be of sound mind and found guilty. The court imposed a sentence of death, which I confirmed. However, higher allied military authority reduced the sentence to life imprisonment without right of parole, which the new Italian government undertook to carry out in its penal system.

Despite this commitment, in December 1964 when she was 51 years old, Maria Pasquinelli received from the president of the Italian republic what the rhapsodizing Italian press referred to as a "pardon." When I passed this news to Lord Harding, who had reduced her sentence to life imprisonment, he commented, "I wouldn't fight her release, but no assassin should be *pardoned*."

Ten days after Robin de Winton's death, the Venezia Giulia Police Force arrested in Trieste a man who declared that, pursuant to agreement with Maria Pasquinelli, he had engaged to do to me in Trieste what she had done to Robin in Pola, and on the same day. I was saved by the fact that business had required my presence in Caserta and Rome when the blow was to have been struck.

In my diary under the date of February 5, arguing with myself about the necessity for the trip that General Lee had urged but not commanded, I had written: "On the other hand, 10 February will be treaty-signing day, and will probably produce some disturbances in Trieste. If I take off for the south I am quite likely not to have returned by that time, and may miss the fun!"

During the Rome portion of that same brief journey, my friend and former chief, Col. Norman Fiske, told me at dinner at the Villa Madama that he planned to live in California after retirement and was determined to see that I ran for governor of that state. Obviously, he didn't know much about California politics or, for that matter about *any* politics. I may win lasting credit in many parts of the world for the job I tried to do in Trieste, but I knew then that this fact would be of no help in the political climate of California. Anyhow, the Colonel's companion, Fanny Caprini, God bless her, said she would have no part of it. She said I was a legend and that a legend should be happy being just that and never run for office. What a wise woman!

On the way home, I stopped in Florence for one night and spent the second night with my family in Venice, so that I could attend the de Winton funeral in Udine the following day without backtracking from Trieste. I found Venice filling up with correspondents on hand for the war crimes trial of Field Marshal Albert Kesselring, which was to take place there later in the week. He was convicted and sentenced to death by the military court, but General Harding reduced the death sentence to life imprisonment.

Except for the continued work of the Economic Commission, the rest of February was virtually blacked out by blizzard conditions that reached their peak on the very day I arrived in Pola via destroyer, accompanied by Generals Harding, Lee, and Moore. The problem that occasioned the trip was the excessive dismantling of industrial facilities as part of the exodus from Pola and a satisfactory adjustment was accomplished, as I have related elsewhere.

In March, we all forced ourselves to get down to the brass tacks of preparing for events that we were told were virtually upon us but, to us workers in the vineyard, still seemed uncertain and far away. One such matter was the preparing of suitable office space and living accommodations for the governor who, under the terms of the still-unratified Treaty of Peace with Italy, would be arriving within a few months.

The Palazzo del Governo, appropriately named, though we usually called it simply the Prefettura or Area Headquarters, seemed the easy choice. It was a building of great dignity, solid, substantial, and not totally unbeautiful, fronting on the great Piazza Unita with its south side facing the Riva and the harbor beyond. It had spacious and gracious accommodations for residence as well as business, although it was in rather rundown condition after a war and occupation by some AMG officers who were not much concerned about niceties. There seemed to be no problem of any consequence.

Another matter, which had been confided to me personally for determination, caused me more concern. Article 8 of Annex VI of the treaty (denominated "Permanent Statute of the Free Territory of Trieste") provided: "The Free Territory shall have its own flag and coat-of-arms. The flag shall be the traditional flag of the City of Trieste, and the arms shall be its historic coat-of-arms."

The problem was that, according to my research, the traditional and historic flag and coat-of-arms bore gold crowns superimposed on the shield and halberd that constituted the main part of both. Eventually I took a chance and eliminated the crowns. This was a clear violation of the letter of the treaty but so far as I know no one has to this day raised the issue.

A negative and sometimes frightening aspect of the winding down process lay in the fact that after the foreign ministers signed the treaty there was a strong tendency on the part of all the people on whom we depended for men, money, and material, to assume that the wind-down was an accomplished fact. Late in March, following a staff meeting, I wrote in my diary:

> One of the greatest problems worrying the staff is what we are going to do if there is not some indication very soon of ratification and the coming of the long-heralded Governor . . . I have a feeling that our busiest and most troublesome times may still lie ahead. It is a little frightening that the attitude of the rest of the world seems to be "well, now Venezia Giulia has been disposed of. Let's go home." One after another we are being deprived of our tools. The Combined Chiefs of Staff seem to feel that we don't even need food. G–5 doesn't like to approve funds now for more public works, even though a lot of people need jobs and will promote unrest if idle. [G–5 is the official designation of the General Staff element of a large Army headquarters (in this case, Allied Force Headquarters at Caserta in southern Italy) that deals with military government and civil affairs.]

AIS [Allied Information Service, postwar successor to the wartime Psychological Warfare Board] has been contracted almost to the point of uselessness. The circumstances are quite different from those in the early days two years ago when everyone knew the situation was critical and pitched in to help.

On the day this was written I drove a pick through a last thin curtain of rock to open a pedestrian tunnel through the base of San Giusto Hill, which greatly facilitated foot traffic between portions of the city that had theretofore been isolated from each other for practical day-to-day purposes. The workers gave me a suitably engraved silver dish as a souvenir, which I can see from where I write these words.

Because I was in middle life an avid horseman, as I am even now a dedicated bicyclist, riding was my sole form of exercise during my time in Trieste, and I tried to ride for an hour or so at some time during every day. As I have said elsewhere, I was never threatened in any way on these equestrian jaunts, despite ideal conditions for ambush. Perhaps I was guarded better than I thought or will ever know. Neither had I ever, in almost two years, ever had an accident of any kind until one afternoon early in April when some loose dirt brought my horse down on a slight rise, and I fell, striking my head on a rock and knocking myself out. This was inhibiting for a few days, which included the opening phases of the firing of the rector of the University of Trieste.

Perhaps if I had not received that temporarily disabling blow, I would have realized sooner than I did that total incompetence as an administrator was not valid or adequate justification for firing a university president. My education officer had apprised me of the unquestioned facts, and I had checked them out weeks and months earlier. Angelo E. Cammarata was a nice man and a noted scholar, of super-irredentist political and ethnic persuasion. But the record showed that he was completely incapable of grasping administrative concepts, to say nothing of applying them effectively to the problems with which the university was confronted in its day-to-day operations. There seemed only one thing to do. Without consulting higher authority, I fired him, with a short statement for the press that I had done so for purely administrative reasons that in no way reflected on his reputation as a scholar and teacher.

Within days I was overwhelmed with telegrams and letters of protest and excoriation from universities and their populations all over the world, including some in Yugoslavia, where Cammarata was well known as a totally unreconstructed chauvinistic irredentist. The messages I received directly were augmented in spades by messages to the Italian ambassador, the State Department, and the president of the United States. The letters were followed by a flock of correspondents, all asking me why I had decided to stifle academic freedom in Venezia Giulia. The local papers had a field day—particularly the satirical *Caleidoscopio*, which printed a full page, highly imaginative account of how, in an interview, I had acknowledged having fired the pope "for administrative reasons."

It was at this juncture that I received the ultimate gift that a subordinate in trouble can receive from a superior. As I have mentioned elsewhere in this account, General Harding informed higher headquarters that he had been fully informed in advance about my action and fully approved it. This relieved the worst of the heat—the part that came from my direct military superiors who might otherwise have made their own discomfort a reason for making my life in the army a lot tougher than it had been. In the end, after several conferences with me and a suggestion that if he continued to sign papers for the university AMG might find it necessary to cut off its financial help, Cammarata departed quietly. However, some historical accounts I have read recently refer to him as the rector of the university in 1949. I assume he was rehired sometime after my departure from the scene.

The communist Labor Day on May 1 was marked by the usual pro-Yugoslav demonstration in the Piazza Unità, but this time without harassment or disorder, due to some effective planning and execution by the now mature and professional Venezia Giulia Police Force, of which I was by this time indeed very proud; however, that sentiment may have been derided by my friends of the press.

The rest of the month was devoted more to the Cammarata affair than to anything else. During that month, I played surrogate father of the bride and other roles in connection with marriages of local girls to several of our enlisted men—both British and American. On May 21, after meeting in Rome with a peripatetic committee from the State Department with a view to possibly joining the Foreign Service, I drove my own jeep back to Trieste in one day—a distance of 550 miles. I have driven greater distances without sleep before and since, but never under conditions as primitive.

During this month also, tensions having lessened, the policy ban on my family living in Trieste was lifted and all five of them joined me. This gave me an opportunity, among burgeoning rumors that I would soon be relieved, to let them see a little of the milieu in which I had lived and worked during two very exciting years. I took them boating in a small requisitioned sailboat that I had long before named the Lari Jane for my daughter. We rode horses together through the hills, and they accompanied me to several of the village reopening and key-delivery ceremonies that were becoming epidemic at about this time.

Also, perhaps motivated in part by the rumors of my impending departure, the press became kinder. At my press conference on May 27, they presented me with a gavel symbolizing my part in the institution that had thrown us together each week during the preceding two years. On the 29th, my friendly persecutors and caricaturists at *La Cittadella* wrote a long feature article, titled "The Bowman Case," which said, in part:

> He says that we are frequently concerned with him. That is a fact and it is easy to explain. We are still young . . . and only a few years ago we were not only totally unaware of Alfred C. Bowman's rather important existence, but had only a very vague idea of America and the Americans themselves. Now we have come to know America. Not through information gathered by us on the spot . . . but through the medium of America's sons. To us, Alfred C. Bowman *is* America with its 48 states, Arizona, William Powell, and Lucky Strike.

I took no offense.

There are few forces more inexorable than army personnel policy, once expressed in a directive. The time for my return home, based on all normal criteria, had really arrived in the fall of 1945, as I was just getting started at Trieste. The urgent protests of my superiors to Washington at that time and again in the spring of 1946, based on operational necessity, had kept me in my challenging role far beyond any reasonable alloted span.

Even in the spring of 1947, although I was unaware of them, similar representations were made again, this time to General

Eisenhower, who was by then army chief of staff. I was honored by having the message of refusal carried from Ike to General Harding by Gen. Omar Bradley. It happened at the Rome airport, where an old friend happened to be present and overheard and reported the exchange. General Harding, wounded in the left hand in battle, has only a thumb and little finger on that hand. When given the negative word, he said to General Bradley, "You know, General, I have a crippled left hand. Now you and General Eisenhower have taken my right arm." Those words alone, from that man, would be worth two years of any soldier's life.

When General Harding told me what the answer was (though he did not tell me the messenger, the circumstances, or his comment), we agreed that I should bow out gracefully. After all, the treaty had been signed and awaited only one or two residual ratifications that were almost certain to come soon. It would go into effect within less than four months. The pattern of the future seemed clear, and the territory was relatively tranquil. The announcment of my forthcoming departure was made on June 10. On the following day, my entire military staff gathered in one place for the first time, for a group picture. The 12th was the second anniversary of our administration. The 13th was a Friday, but a good day despite this. At my final press conference, the regulars present signed their names on the large softwood gavel they had given me a fortnight earlier.

My departure was the signal for a great spate of editorial comment by the local press. Characteristically, if perhaps somewhat sacrilegiously, the issue of *La Cittadella* published the same day as the press conference, portrayed me as the central figure at a Last Supper—"In order that the scriptures may be fulfilled." I have never quite grasped the metaphor, but indeed for the next week there was a last supper or dinner or lunch of some kind every day. It was all very heartwarming and was to be repeated four years later when I returned briefly on an inspection trip as chief of the army's Military Government Division.

Members of the local press responded in accordance with the various ideologies and points of view they represented, but in general they were kind to me. Their comments were summarized in the news columns of the 88th Infantry Division's newspaper, the *Blue Devil*, also under dateline of Friday the 13th:

The news of Colonel Bowman's imminent departure for the States was front page news for the local press. In addition, all of the local newspapers carried editorials on the subject.

All Trieste newspapers have strong political convictions, and these were not lacking in the editorial comments on the departure of the AMG chief. Since the Peace Conference solution of the Trieste problem pleased neither Italy nor Jugoslavia, it followed that their adherents regularly took affront at Colonel Bowman personally as he carried out his duty of implementing the policies laid down for him. Their editorials about his departure were quite temperate, however, and generally paid tribute to "Bowman, the man and the soldier." All wished him happiness.

To the Communist press, led by *Il Lavoratore*, Colonel Bowman has been, of course, anathema, since he is not pro-Communist. In its editorial, "Farewell To Bowman," it attacks the system he represents, but also says, "Rightly Gen. Harding says of him that nothing prevented him from doing his duty . . . He did his duty as a soldier." They also state that they wish that in California in his civil life all may go for the best.

Giornale di Trieste, a middle-of-the-road pro-Italian newspaper which, like others in the same category, failed to understand his American-like treatment of the rights of racial and political minorities here, treated the Colonel as two personalities: Bowman as man and Bowman as Chief of the AMG. For the latter, they had bitter words for the administrator of Allied Civil Affairs policy. For the former, they had very kind words, including as fine a tribute as any American could ever hope to have when they stated he "serves his flag against all and beyond everything."

All the papers failed to realize, in their editorials, the tremendous job AMG has done, under Colonel Bowman's leadership, of helping to bring Trieste far forward on the road to economic recovery; the constructive things that have been accomplished under his administration; the efficient police force built from the ground up in a year and a half, which *Newsweek* recently stated is "said to be the best in Central Europe."

I am afraid it was not quite accurate to say that all elements of the press wished me a happy future. The pro-Yugoslav *Primorski Dnevnik*'s comment in its issue of June 12 seemed to brook no such nonsense:

Trieste, 12 June 1947

Farewell to Col. Bowman

Col. Bowman, who at the end of the war against Nazi-Fascism arrived in Trieste and personified the policy of AMG is about to return to civil life. The attitude our people adopted with regard to his policy is not likely to undergo any change in the future.

Today is the second anniversary of the instatement of AMG in this region. [The] balance sheet of these two years is not a happy one. Our fundamental problems were not solved. After two years of "democratic" manoeuvres against anti-Fascist forces, an offensive of joint reactionary and Fascist groups was launched in an attempt to disparage the reputation of anti-Fascist organisations.

These are the results of "sympathy" the Allies felt towards our people and the respect they had for the tremendous war efforts we developed during the war. We are being reproached by certain elements to have adopted the attitude which cost us this "sympathy." The same thing, however, happened to other staunch anti-Fascist fighters in Greece and China. American tanks are being sent against them today. Yugoslavia, Albania, Bulgaria, Rumania, Poland, Czechoslovakia, and Hungary are no longer favoured by the Allies. Unable to send tanks to these countries, America sends them protest notes and organises slander campaigns against them. Hirelings are set to work in the territories where the Americans cannot reach. This activity represents defamation of the sacrifices brought by the American people during the war. Servants of reactionaries work hard. In difficult moments they are propped up by eulogies. Prominent persons do not spare compliments which inspire servants with a new zeal.

We are not to be blamed for the fact that the same tanks, which were during the war used against Fascists, are directed against Anti-Fascists today.

Not one single request with regard to introduction of equal rights to both languages was granted so far. The problems of Slovene schools, cultural institutions, Slovene National Theatre, untenable economic conditions on those of our workmen who are lucky enough to be employed, are far from being solved.

We are not affected by the loss of your "sympathies." We shall manage to get along without them. We shall never sell our anti-Fascist creed for a plate of lentils.

This is our farewell to Col. Bowman in a few plain words. We wish Col. Bowman for the sake of his spiritual harmony to have no doubts about the part he played during the time he ruled Trieste.

Finally, I said goodbye to the Triestini in a speech delivered from a local radio station:

> I am happy to be afforded this opportunity, through the invitation of Radio Trieste, to say a few words of farewell to the people of British/American–occupied Venezia Giulia, whose problems have provided me, in the position of senior civil affairs officer, with the busiest and most completely absorbing two years of my life.
>
> I am sorry to leave you. This is said quite sincerely though it causes some of my friends to raise an eyebrow, in view of the history of strife, criticism, and disagreement between you and me during my incumbency here.
>
> With all its difficulties and wearisome labor, the administration of Allied Military Government in Venezia Giulia has afforded me more real, lasting pleasure than anything else I have ever done, and a great

deal of this pleasure has been based on my intimate day-to-day acquaintance with you—your lives, problems, and aspirations. I shall miss you very much.

And I hope that a few of you will miss me, too, and regret my departure. This might have seemed a vain hope a few weeks ago, but I have been greatly gratified and encouraged by the messages I have received since the announcement of my imminent departure, the general tenor of which from every source is that, while I made many mistakes—all, of course, from the standpoint of the individual writer—I was at least honest, impartial, and kind.

Through it all, you must believe, I have never ceased, within the prescribed limits of my mission, to be deeply concerned about your welfare, prosperity, and happiness. I think that "when the tumult and the shouting die" and you are able to direct your energies again principally to those workaday problems that consitute normalcy in most places and that will one day, I hope, have like significance in Trieste, you will have time to contemplate these things. I ask that you then compare your condition with that of the rest of the world and decide—dispassionately and with undistorted perspective—whether Allied Military Government tried to help you and to what degree it succeeded in doing so. I have confidence in your verdict at that time.

In other words, I love you—all of you—and wish you very well. I understand your aspirations and hope that they may all be fulfilled to the highest possible degree consistent with the similar realization of the hopes of your neighbors and fellow-townsmen. This is the essence of true Democracy.

I hope that you and yours will, in the years to come, find solutions to the many problems that now beset you and that you will find complete happiness.

With all my heart, I wish it.

And if, when you do, you should occasionally look and think back kindly on the American colonel who lived with you through these troubled past two years, my cup of joy will be full.

I shall be thinking of you!

Good-bye. Good luck. Godspeed and (I hope) arrivederci.

In approving the text for delivery in Italian, my public relations officer scribbled at the bottom of the last page of the script some words that I still cherish: "If the opportunity had been mine, I would be very proud of such a speech for the unwritten spirit behind each word clearly indicates the speaker's belief in his job as a human need fulfilled in good faith under difficult circumstances when great trust had to be centered in one individual."

Friends, associates, and professional readers of this account have questioned my expression in my farewell speech of love for the people of all political persuasions who had caused me so much trouble and concern during my incumbency in Trieste; some have even expressed skepticism as to my sincerity. To these I say first of all: there's no explaining love. When I spoke the questioned words, their purport was known only to me, and I reassert their accuracy and sincerity.

Beyond this, I refer to a few pregnant words of an obscure poet, Robert D. Abrahams, a Philadelphia lawyer, whose words in this as in other respects have had a very pronounced influence on my life: "Adventure shared is most of love." So it has been with me, whatever be the road to love for others. The two years just ended had been full of high adventure shared with the people of Trieste and Venezia Giulia, however diverse the points of view and means of expression of the participants.

Looking back on those two years and the disorders they had witnessed, it seemed to me that I perceived a sort of innocent sincerity on the part of both of the factions that had contributed to my problems. Despite the headlines around the world, there had been very little true violence and very few deaths. No buildings had been bombed, no cars overturned and set afire. Each of the contending factions had expressed its sincerely held views in massive demonstrations. Despite the exasperation my course of action caused on both sides, no one had sought to injure me physically, although there had been ample opportunity and political excuse.

Beyond this, which seems to me remarkable, no local person had tried to corrupt me—a circumstance most remarkable in a situation where one man exercises great de facto power over others. I had dealt with business leaders and political leaders in private as well as publicly. In no case during those two years did I ever feel that the men who confronted me or sought to influence my action were less than completely sincere in the points of view they expressed, and not one of them ever made any effort to influence my action by the offer of a gift of any sort. The one exception to this remarkable record, considering the circumstances, was that of a regular British officer and former associate, in civilian life by 1947, who would have rewarded me for helping to turn Trieste into another Monte Carlo or Adriatic Reno.

To those who say these matters are cause for approval or admiration rather than love, I say, "so be it." Beyond all such matters, the truth lies in my heart. When I said "I love you" to the people of Trieste, I reported a fact. And if I said it today, it would still be a fact, which I now happily reassert.

In all candor, had I been called upon for a similiar farewell address a month later, I might have excluded from the Dearly Beloved category at least some of my friendly enemies of the press.

While I was engaged in the business described in the chapter that follows, a police investigation originally aimed at the discovery and extirpation of local civilian corruption disclosed that two of my most trusted and effective officers had accepted gifts of money from civilian contractors following the award of public works contracts to the donors. I had been advised during the last days of my incumbency of a change in the direction of the investigation that might involve AMG personnel and had directed that the new lines of inquiry be pursued the more diligently because our own house was involved.

In midsummer, while I was on a trip to central Europe and England, some of the local papers speculated in print, without any basis whatever in disclosed facts, that I might have been a participant in the corruption. I was and remain quite confident that none of them really believed this, and *La Voce Libera*, one of my most consistent critics, was gracious enough to say so even while bearing down on me for other sins. If any doubt remained, it was quickly dissipated when I returned to Trieste, submitted myself to examination (followed by an apology from the prosecutor), and asked for an investigation by the inspector general of the Army.

Czech Interlude

Presenting "A Bell for Barbana"

One day in late June 1947, my wife and I, accompanied by my most recent personal assistant who was also going home, headed for the Alps and points north in a borrowed automobile. One objective was yet to be achieved. Although I had been on the European continent for four years, I had never left the Italian peninsula and adjacent foothills of the Austrian Alps except for a brief operational and educational foray to Vienna and Munich in the fall of 1945.

Also, the government of Czechoslovakia, unlike Yugoslavia's leaders, felt that I had done a good job in expediting the unloading and delivery of UNRRA supplies and had invited me to come to Prague to receive a military decoration in recognition of this achievement.

While we were in Vienna, awaiting issuance by the Russians of a pass through the Soviet zone of occupied Austria, I noted an ominous headline in the *New York Herald-Tribune*, European edition, of July 3, 1947. It concerned Secretary of State George C. Marshall's proposal for the economic reconstruction of Europe.

> PARIS PARLEY ON AID ENDS IN FAILURE
> AS MOLOTOV REJECTS WESTERN PROPOSAL
> BUT BRITAIN, FRANCE, ARE CONTINUING
>
> POWERS TRADE WARNINGS AND THREATS
> AS FINAL EAST-WEST SPLIT NEARS

I was relieved to note in the same journal's edition of the following day, that:

> BRITAIN AND FRANCE INVITE 22 COUNTRIES
> TO TAKE ACTION ON MARSHALL PROPOSALS
> AT CONFERENCE OPENING IN PARIS JULY 12

Before I could catch my breath in Prague the next day, we were whisked off to the Tatra foothills by the Czech public relations people to observe the Jan Hus Day celebrations. On our return, the news was much better:

> CZECHS AGREE TO COME TO PARIS TALKS
> ON PLAN POLES AND FINNS WAVER
>
> EVEN NATIONS IN SOVIET ORBIT
> BEGIN TO LEAN TOWARDS WEST

> AP Prague, July 7: The Czech government decided in a closed session today to accept the invitation to the Paris conference on the Marshall proposal despite Soviet rejection of the original proposals.
> The decision was taken on the eve of the delayed departure of Prime Minister Gottwald and Foreign Minister Jan Masaryk, and without waiting for results of their talks with Russian Foreign Minister Vyacheslav M. Molotov.
> Because the Paris conference begins too soon for Mr. Masaryk to reach there on his return from Moscow, the government decided that the Czech representative at the start of the conference would be the Czech ambassador Jundrich Nosak, in Paris. Mr. Masaryk will take over as soon as he can get there from Moscow.

While this was very interesting, I had other problems, which were causing me some embarrassment. The public relations officer who was our full-time guide and keeper let it be known that I was expected to call on both the American ambassador and the Czech foreign minister. I had no personal objection to this, but was embarrassed by my total lack at that time of any official status that would justify my association with ambassadors and ministers. In Europe, clearly, I was a has-been.

However, since there seemed no way to avoid the issue short of asserting an unworthiness I did not really feel, I asked my hosts to make a date for me with Jan Masaryk, the foreign minister, on the afternoon of the following day. Then I used the telephone myself to arrange an interview with our ambassador during the morning of the same day.

Laurence Steinhardt proved no problem at all. He seemed almost eagerly glad to see me and happily expounded on the perquisites and posts I should seek during the foreign service career I was then considering. In an hour, plus time on my way out to apologize to the U.S. Army attaché for having (contrary to army protocol) called the ambassador direct, that part of the job was done. It was easy.

I felt much less at ease at 6:00 P.M. when I was led up two flights of ancient stone steps in the Czernin Palace on the banks of the Charles River, ushered into an outer room of the minister's private apartment, and told he would join me there.

I waited, alone, for about forty minutes. Just as I was about to conclude that there must have been a mistake, at least about the time, a man with the oval, cherubic face I recognized from many newspaper pictures entered the room. After gripping my hand firmly, Jan Masaryk dropped into a big, ornate, swivel chair, and swung both feet up on top of a richly-carved medieval desk. Incongruously, in the Graustarkian surroundings, he wore a poison-green knit-rayon shirt, and his light brown slacks were supported by both a red cloth belt and purple suspenders—more or less the standard lower middle-class leisure garb that was customary back home in 1940.

I'm able to reconstruct our conversation from my vivid memories of the occasion and my diary entries.

"Well, Colonel," he said, "I've been following your career of crime. How did you leave Trieste? Did you like my country?"

"Your people couldn't have been kinder, Mr. Minister," I replied. "We celebrated Jan Hus in the mountains over the weekend. Yesterday, your army chief of staff pinned me with your Military Medal of Merit (for which I thank you) and we visited Lidice and your father's farm. Today I called on Mr. Steinhardt and had lunch with your working delegates to the Marshall Plan talks that will start Saturday in Paris. If the delegates from everywhere else are as steamed up about the Marshall Plan as yours seem to be, it has a great future."

"You said it, brother!"

Although I knew that his mother had been born in Brooklyn, and that he had spent much of his youth in the United States, he was even more aggressively and colloquially American than I had expected.

"It will be a wonderful thing for Czechoslovakia, although frankly we may not need the help, as such, as much as some other nations. Basically we're in better balance: small population, plenty of food, and most of our industrial plant in fair condition. But as a token of our stance in relation to the West... You know, Bowman, Will Clayton and Stettinius still doubt we'll come to Paris at all. They're afraid Johnny can't swing it, but they're wrong. But what about your personal plans? I understand you're not a regular officer. What next?"

"I'll probably end up back where the war picked me up—as a reserve officer practicing law on Spring Street in Los Angeles," I told him. "However, I may get into your business. The State Department is recruiting a few wartrained old-timers—AMG and such—for service in what it calls the middle and upper brackets. I'm on the eligible list."

"Don't do it, Bowman. Even if you're lucky, it's a fool's game. Look where it's got me. Of course, in my case it can't be helped. My father invented this country, and I've got to stay with it—and want to. You say you visited the old homestead yesterday?"

"Yes, sir."

"Thomas Masaryk was a very great man, Colonel. This nation he dreamed up has been and will continue to be a very good thing—long term—in spite of a lot of baloney we've been hearing recently about the glorious Old Empire. There's a new brand of baloney going the rounds now, however, about the Iron Curtain. You seem to have surveyed the country pretty well. Have you seen the Iron Curtain?"

"Mr. Masaryk, we've been so surrounded and overwhelmed with attention by your public relations staff that we wouldn't be able to see an Iron Curtain ten feet away. However, the fact that everyone here asks the same question makes us wonder whether you, yourselves, are really sure the curtain isn't there. You know: Methinks he doth protest too much."

"Bowman, that is the toughest part of my job. What you just said is substantially what Will Clayton thinks—in special application to the Paris Conference. I have to cope with it every day. Maybe in your case I can prevent suspicion from hardening into conviction. I guess you know that I'm half American myself . . . My mother . . ."

"You certainly talk like homefolks."

"And you probably think that helps me in my work. Well, in a way it does. I can talk to Marshall and Stettinius and the rest of you Americans in your own language. It makes things much easier—to the West.

"But of course here on the East Forty we have more than the West to think about. We always have had. You mentioned Jan Hus. Five hundred years ago, the Hussites were impaled on the horns of the same dilemma, and the situation hasn't changed much, in any essential respect.

"The problem is no monopoly of our country, either. While I hate to mention Germany in the same breath as my own country, they've got it, too. In fact, so long as you and England stick together, *all* central European nations are bound to be buffer states. But it's tougher for this country because we're Slavs. And it's toughest of all for me because I *did* go to school in the States, and talk like an American, and my mother *was* one. That's no background for a central European diplomat, Bowman."

"How could it be better? A Slav, educated in the United States and the son of the national hero—the father of his country . . ."

"That's a very superficial evaluation, Bowman. Each of the attributes you mentioned carries with it the seed of its own frustration. To begin with: at this point in history, you can't expect Americans to trust any Slav fully. And to the Slavs that count most (I'm going to fly over to see them tomorrow), any fellow Slav that speaks English fluently is suspect. Being my father's son is not all beer and skittles, either. Dad could pull rabbits out of a hat, and I suffer from the usual comparisons between great fathers and less gifted offspring.

"However, don't get me wrong. It's tough, but I've got it licked, if I can just keep the confidence of my American friends; if they'll only understand that a tightrope is not a suspension bridge. As a lawyer, Bowman, you know that you can't settle a dispute by inducing one side to make all the concessions, even if you know that in good conscience they should do just that. You have to engage in give-and-take, even when your heart and your convictions are all on one side.

"That's what I've been trying to get over to Will Clayton during the past couple of years. So far, I've been able to make my point, though the margin has been narrow at times. But if your people and the British will have faith and stick with me a little while longer, we'll have it made.

"And this European Recovery Plan is the very thing that's going to clinch it. Bowman, we're not only going to be in Paris next Saturday, we're going to be in there pitching. We're not only going to join the club; we're also going to propose some new members from among our neighbors—maybe not right away, but soon. When they see what it does for us, that is. Bowman, do you realize what a radical, unprecedented, inspired thing this Marshall Plan is? There has never in all history been anything even remotely approaching it for pure, inspired vision."

"I'm a long-term optimist myself, Mr. Minister, and I believe you're right."

"You're damn right I'm right, Bowman. It's all over but the shouting. You had lunch today with the people who are doing it—the 'Indians,' as they say in the Pentagon. Is there any doubt in your mind about the determination and confidence of these people concerning the job they have to do next week in Paris, or here in the months to come? Did they hold back on you? Did you sense any Iron Curtain between you and them, either today or while you were helping them to bring in those UNRRA supplies through the Port of Trieste?"

"The answer is 'No' to all questions, Mr. Masaryk."

"Right. When do you plan to leave?"

"Tomorrow. We're going to drive down to the American zone of Germany. We'll have lunch and a Pilsener at Pilsen and be in Nuremberg tomorrow night."

"I'm going the other way, as I told you. By noon tomorrow, I'll be in Moscow. And I suppose my American friends will all be in a stew about it. They needn't, Bowman. These things I have to do, but remember I told you: it's in the bag. If there were going to be any strong objections from that quarter, I'd have heard them long since. This is a routine trip—strictly protocol. So when you see General Marshall . . ."

"Mr. Minister, I'm a colonel and, as you pointed out, a reserve officer. I won't see General Marshall."

"Maybe so. Then I won't give you any message for him. But remember what I said when you get back to Los Angeles and read that another $10 million worth of machinery has been consigned to Prague. Good bye, now."

I was ushered out.

Next day, we found the Pilsener beer as represented, and entered the American zone of Germany about mid-afternoon. We stayed the night at Nuremberg and on the following morning called on old friends who were sitting as judges in the second-generation war crimes trials. Late in the afternoon, we found our Los Angeles friends at their quarters in Stuttgart, ready to take off with us for Paris.

This was Friday, July 11, but we didn't see the Paris papers until the following morning:

CZECHS REFUSE PARIS INVITATION AFTER LEADERS
REACH MOSCOW; SIXTEEN NATIONS NOW EXPECTED

GOTTWALD AND MASARYK TALK
WITH STALIN BEFORE DECISION

Paris, July 10: Czechoslovakia reversed her previous acceptance of the invitation to the Paris Conference on the Marshall proposal and announced last night that she would not be among the nations which will gather at the French Ministry of Foreign Affairs at 11 o'clock tomorrow morning. The reversal of her decision came after the Czech Premier and Foreign Minister had been received Wednesday night in the Kremlin by Premier Joseph V. Stalin.

By her refusal, Czechoslovakia joined the ranks of four other countries within the sphere of Soviet influence from whom the French government had received refusals. They are Poland, Roumania, Yugoslavia, and Bulgaria.

The Cold War, second phase, had begun.

Exactly eight months later, to the day, the *Washington Daily News* carried the story of the tragic denouement as it related to the personal fate of the euphoric subject of my interview:

MASARYK, CZECH HERO, KILLS SELF

Prague, March 10: Foreign Minister Jan Masaryk, 61, one of Czechoslovakia's distinguished statesmen, killed himself today by plunging three stories from the bathroom window of his official residence in Czernin Palace.

Members of the family said his suicide was in protest against the Communist coup in Czechoslovakia. The son of the founder of the republic, while calling himself a political independent, had accepted reappointment to the Foreign Ministry.

Interior Minister Maclov Nasek told the opening session of the purged parliament that Dr. Masaryk went from his bedroom to the bathroom about 6 a.m. and from there leaped into the courtyard.

Some hours after the suicide, the government issued a formal statement which said that Dr. Masaryk evidently decided in a moment of nervous breakdown to end his life. The statement mentioned illness and insomnia, but did not elaborate on the reference.

Dr. Masaryk, the official statement said, showed no evidence of mental depression yesterday and last night, on the contrary evincing his "usual optimism."

Twenty years later, the writer Marcia Davenport, who had been in Prague and enjoyed a close personal relationship with Mr. Masaryk at the time (although I did not know this then), confirmed the accuracy of the foregoing account as a portrayal of his manner and views at the time.

Retrospect and Prospect

While waiting for family shipment home: with Major Fred Blanchard (custodian of American dependents at the Venice Lido) in the Venetian Regatta, a parade and display of gondolas and other craft

Meanwhile, at the head of the Adriatic, events were not going according to plan. From the beginning, it had been apparent that the success of the solution for the Trieste problem, adopted on Maria Pasquinelli's big day, would depend in high degree not only on the personality, character, and administrative ability of the governor, but also on the degree of confidence accorded him by the U.N. Security Council. During the months before I had set off for Prague, we at AMG had devoted primary attention to providing facilities and services that would enable him to get about his difficult business promptly following his arrival, which we had assumed would be more or less concurrent with the effective date of the Treaty of Peace with Italy on September 15, 1947.

On the other hand, the possibility that some time-lag between the effective date of the treaty and the arrival of the governor had been foreseen was reflected in the language of Article I of Annex VII of the treaty. This article specifically provided that "pending the assumption of office by the governor" the Free Territory should continue to be administered in the same manner as had been done since June 1945. During this interim period and for 90 days after the governor's assumption of the office, he would have at his disposal in the Free Territory 15,000 troops, provided in equal numbers by the United States, Great Britain, and Yugoslavia.

When I returned in August from France, England, and Germany to the Adriatic littoral (specifically, to the American Family Center at the Venice Lido, which had been my family's home during the preceding hectic year), I learned that the situation that had prevailed when I left for Prague remained virtually unchanged. Since in those days families were literally shipped, my family and I had to wait for a suitable transport vessel until mid-October. Hence, I continued for sometime to be a spectator, at rather close geographical range, to the drama in which I had recently played a major part.

On or soon after September 15, a small party of American congressmen arrived in Venice. They were members of the Herter party, under Chairman Christian Herter, and were charged with sizing up the condition of war-wracked Europe for U.S. legislative purposes, especially as these related to the Marshall Plan. I was required not only to brief them about Trieste up to the time of my departure but also, as the senior American present, to show them around Venice.

On one of the days they were in my care I thought it appropriate to top off the day's work with a little indigenous innocent entertainment of string music and folk dancing. I admit having been impressed when, at about 10 P.M., freshman Congressman Richard Milhous Nixon turned to his very senior colleagues and said "Let's turn in, fellahs. We've got work to do tomorrow."

Well, no governor arrived at Trieste on September 15, or on any day thereafter. The steadily deteriorating sense of rapport and common purpose between the wartime allies and administrative measures, contrary to the intent of the Free Territory Statute that had been put into effect in the Yugoslav-controlled segment, created an impasse in the Security Council discussions regarding the selection of a governor. On March 20, 1948, long after my family and I had at last gone home and ten days after the suicide or murder of Jan Masaryk, the conflicts remained unresolved. On that day the governments of the United States, the United Kingdom, and France proposed to the governments of the Soviet Union and Italy that an additional protocol be added to the treaty of peace, which would again place Trieste under Italian sovereignty. The tripartite proposal stated:

> The Governments of the United States, United Kingdom and France have come to this decision because discussions in the Security Council have already shown that an agreement on the selection of a governor is impossible, and because they have received abundant evidence to show that the Yugoslav Zone has been completely transformed in character and has been virtually incorporated into Yugoslavia by procedures which do not respect the desire expressed by the powers to give an independent and democratic status to the territory.
>
> During the Council of Foreign Ministers' discussion of the Italian peace treaty, it was the consistent position of the American, British, and French representatives that Trieste, which has an overwhelmingly Italian population, must remain an Italian city. Given the impossibility of securing the adoption of such a solution, the three Governments agreed that the city and a small hinterland should be established as a Free Territory, under a statute which it was hoped would guarantee, with the cooperation of all parties concerned, the independence of the people of the area, including the Italian city of Trieste.
>
> Pending the assumption of office by a governor, the Free Territory has been administered by the Commander, British-United States Forces in the northern zone of the Territory, and by the Commander, Yugoslav Forces in the southern zone. In the U.K.–U.S. zone the Anglo-American military authorities have acted as caretakers for the governor to be appointed and for the democratic organs of popular representation for which the permanent statute of the Territory makes provision. At the same time, Yugoslavia has taken, in the zone under her charge, measures which definitely compromise the possibility of applying the terms of the statute.
>
> In these circumstances, the three Governments have concluded that the present settlement cannot guarantee the preservation of the basic rights and interests of the people of the Free Territory.
>
> The Governments of the United States, the United Kingdom, and France have therefore decided to recommend the return of the Free Territory of Trieste to Italian sovereignty as the best solution to meet the democratic aspirations of the people, and to make possible the reestablishment of peace and stability in the area.
>
> Inasmuch as the Security Council has assumed responsibility for the independence and territorial integrity of the Free Territory of Trieste, the Governments of the United States, the United Kingdom, and France will submit to the Security Council for its approval the

arrangements to be jointly adopted. (U.S. Department of State, "Recommendation for Return of Free Territory of Trieste to Italy," *Bulletin* [March 28, 1948], p. 425.)

In subsequent discussions of the Trieste question at Lake Success, New York, the British, French, and American delegates continued to press for the return of the Free Territory to Italy.

Eventually, the product of the extraordinary effort and attention reported by President Eisenhower was a Memorandum of Agreement signed by the foreign ministers of the U.N. Security Council member-nations on October 5, 1954. Its effect was to confer upon Italy and Yugoslavia the temporary right, without sovereignty, to administer the west and east zones, respectively, into which the Free Territory of Trieste (the president's "tiny patch of land") was divided.

Contrary to an erroneous impression prevalent in some quarters, this did not in itself put an end to the Free Territory. Thirteen years later, the State Department in an official memorandum transmitted to Senator Thomas H. Kuchel, stated:

> The Free Territory . . . is still a legal entity; should the members of the Security Council agree on the selection of a Governor of the Territory, and on a date for the coming into force of the Permanent Statute of the Free Territory, the remaining provisions of the Italian Peace Treaty relating to Trieste presumably would be carried out. (State Department memorandum, "The Status of Trieste," sent by William B. Macomber, Jr., Assistant Secretary of State for Congressional Relations, November 2, 1967.)

In 1971, as we entered Trieste from Ljubljana, my wife and I for the first time in thirty years of extensive travel in every part of the world crossed an international boundary without encountering a single customs or immigration official on either side of the line. In Trieste, we found that our most ardently Italian friends were routinely driving their power cruisers on weekends and holidays to the Yugoslav ports of the Dalmatian coast. Other friends quite cheerfully characterized their Italian city as an "outpost of the Balkans."

Meanwhile, John Foster Dulles (whose fief in his time was the world, as it later became Henry Kissinger's), and successive American secretaries of state, had continued gently to nudge the two nations further toward contact and conciliation. The eventual fruit of this effort ripened almost 21 years later when Italian Premier Aldo Moro asked his nation's parliament to ratify the Osimo Agreement with Yugoslavia, which would convert the line between the Italian and Yugoslav administrative zones, with minor adjustments, into a permanent international boundary. On November 10, 1975, in ceremonies at Belgrade and Ancona, Italy, the recommended accord was signed by the foreign ministers of the two nations.

A critical side-effect of the agreement was that it forever blasted the hopes of thousands of Italians east of the line (Maria Pasquinelli's prime clients) for eventual reunion with Mother Italy and required them instead to accept abhorrent Slav nationality. "Naturally," said the later-martyred Aldo Moro, "a deep bitterness remains . . . The government fully understands this, but it is our duty to tell the nation we cannot stand still with our sorrow." A Roman told an American reporter: "With this agreement, a beautiful love affair has come to an end."

To many an idealistic protagonist of some kind of permanent world order, another even more precious dream faded on the horizon: the idea of a prototype international state that might be the seed from which world government could grow and flower. If they were required to work together and reach agreement in small matters within the framework of the Little Mouse State, perhaps the nations of the world might eventually learn to collaborate similarly in larger matters affecting world peace. At least, they would get to know one another. At the very least, the Free Territory would have provided a working model for use in similar zones of strain elsewhere. As this is written, the West Bank of the Jordan River and the island of Cyprus come to mind.

One may well ask whether the Osimo Agreement will, as a matter of law, finally abort the United Nations' slow-gestating "first-born" any more effectively than the 1954 Memorandum Agreement. It can certainly be argued with some force that it will not, since the overwhelming majority of the nations that signed the treaty of peace that created the Free Territory of Trieste are not parties to the agreement, unless tacitly. However, whatever the legal position, the indications clearly are that the Security Council has not merely suspended, but finally abandoned, the mission entrusted to it in 1947. As a practical matter, it seems clear that a free territory anywhere is an idea whose brief hour has come and gone for our generation.

And so, rather sadly for well-intentioned and idealistic observers, who yearn for a single commonwealth on spaceship earth, one single glimmer of hope has been obscured. The prestige of the United Nations has slipped another notch, to a point far below what was hoped for it thirty years ago. The Italians and Yugoslavs involved will curse, weep, or applaud according to their personal circumstances. Few people enjoy being guinea pigs, even for very exalted ends.

In an early draft of this memoir, I concluded my work with the words: "And the daily life of the Triestini—those most loveable and excellent people—will go on as usual in the Corso and the Piazzas, in the shadow of San Giusto, but no longer under the Alabardo."

However, recent reports indicate, ironically, that this is not the case. The Osimo Agreement, one of whose presumed prime purposes was to ensure the eternal Italianity of Trieste, has apparently backfired to produce an opposite result. Trieste has become a Mecca for Yugoslav tourists and shoppers, including Yugoslav soldiers on leave. Louis B. Fleming, Rome correspondent for the *Los Angeles Times* News Service, reports that Yugoslavs by the hundreds invade the city daily, chiefly to buy Italian-made western jeans, which they wear several layers deep back across the border for resale in other Eastern European countries, including the USSR. Another highly knowledgeable journalist reports:

> The streets at weekends were crowded with Yugoslav cars and the shops with tourists exploiting the fall of the lira. At the harbour cafe which James Joyce patronised, the old waiters have had to learn words and phrases of Slovene and Serbo-Croat to cope with the orders for coffee and beer.
> In the hill village of Opicina, where Burton had his villa, the Slovenes are prosperous to the point of smugness. The funicular tram on the way back to Trieste was full of uniformed Yugoslav soldiers, taking a night on the town over the frontier, and many former Italian refugees have gone to retire in what is now Yugoslavia.
> The Yugoslavs and Italians may never actually like each other, but each country admits certain qualities in the other. You hear Yugoslavs praise the quality of Italian goods. The Italians admire the rough justice given to hooligans by the Yugoslav police.

> Sitting in a cafe watching the Yugoslav tourists quarrelling with the Italian waiters, it seemed odd that the Trieste crisis, which once threatened to bring about a third world war, should now be reduced to complaints of warm beer.

A lifetime resident and former AIS employee writes, in a letter to the author:

> As far as the local situation is concerned . . . when you walk about Trieste you can hardly hear any Italian spoken (on weekdays) as the place is crowded with buyers from across the border, and the shop-owners mostly employ people who speak both Slovene and Serbo-Croatian. If you happen to go to the marketplace, the stall owners, who are Slovenes from the surrounding area, will talk to you only in Slovene. The great business at present is Western wear, from jeans on, and we hear they reach even the Moscow market.
> The owners of local stores, little by little, are Jugoslavs. The recent Osimo settlement calls for the building of an industrial area on two-thirds of the Trieste Carso, in which the majority of labor should come from various parts of Jugoslavia, expecially Macedonians. Can you imagine the old Trieste in this new world? At first sight, everything here looks prosperous, rich and happy. Let's hope the future has better things in store for Trieste. Right now, the population consists of people above 60 years of age in the majority, and getting older, as young people, the few, run away as soon as they can make it.

President Tito is gone now, and thus far apprehensions of the disintegration of his nation by reason of jealousy and divergence of aspirations between its component republics have not materialized. Serb, Croat, Slovene, Macedonian, Montenegrin, Bosnian, and Herzegovinian seem to be tolerating one another better than many distinguished Yugoslav watchers had freely prophesied.

Another threat, referred to earlier, persists. When troops were needed to aid in the rescue effort following the massive earthquakes in Italy's Mezzogiorno, the *Los Angeles Times* of November 30, 1980, reported that they were slow in coming. "One reason it took them so long was that, by NATO orders, two-thirds of the Italian troops are stationed near the Yugoslav frontier in the north, on the theory that an eventual Soviet invasion will start there. The Italian boot is long."

A 1981 Christmas message I received from Trieste refers nostalgically to the hectic events of which I have written: "Those were the days! At present the Triestini, Friulani, etc., love to read and listen to stories from Franz Joseph and Maria Theresa's times.

They have even founded nostalgia associations throughout the area, so the celebrations of the various anniversaries sound very 'eine zwei.'" A return to the Hapsburgs?

It is perhaps the final irony that the Cold War goes on elsewhere unabated, but apparently no longer in Trieste where it began.

Appendix

Report No. 192

SUBJECT: Report on local government organization in Venezia Giulia.

Persons interviewed:

    Col. Bowman, SCAO XIII Corps AMG

    Col. Robertson, DSCAO XIII Corps AMG

    Lt. Col. Armstrong, Trieste Area Commissioner

    Lt. Col. Kucera, Trieste City Commissioner

    Lt. Col. Orpwood, Pola City Commissioner

    Lt. Col. Smuts, Gorizia Area Commissioner

    Major Gold, Legal Officer, Gorizia Area

TO: Director, Local Government Sub Commission

FROM: Major Ralph R. Temple, Deputy Director, Local Government Sub Commission

1. I arrived in Udine by plane on 26 July 1945, where I was met by automobile which took me to the Headquarters of XIII Corps AMG at Trieste. I reported to Col. Bowman and informed him that I was here to learn what the organization of local government in Venezia Giulia was and to lend whatever assistance I could if it was thought desirable. Col. Bowman informed me that Col. Robertson, DSCAO, had been delegated by him to be in charge of local government matters and that the latter had the problem in hand. He asked me to confer with Col. Robertson.

2. Col. Robertson, whom I saw immediately, suggested that I get the general picture from Lt. Col. Armstrong, Trieste Area Commissioner, whom he would telephone and that the next day he would discuss the situation with me while driving down to Pola. He asked me to accompany him on this trip.

3. I therefore conferred with Lt. Col. Armstrong on Thursday, 26 July, and on Friday, 27 July, accompanied Col. Robertson to Pola, where we conferred with Lt. Col. Orpwood on the Pola local government situation.

4. On Saturday morning, 28 July, I attended the general staff conference presided over by Col. Bowman. One matter involving Patriots was

raised and Major Henderson, Patriot Officer, was instructed to confer with me. I have since discussed this matter with Major Reakes of this S/C.

5. In the afternoon of Saturday, 28 July, I conferred with Col. Robertson who showed me a plan of local government organization that the Legal Officer on the staff of Lt. Col. Smuts, Gorizia Area Commissioner, had prepared. I indicated to Col. Robertson that I did not think it adequate and volunteered to draw up a more comprehensive scheme of government. Col. Robertson accepted the invitation and we discussed generally what the plan should embrace. I borrowed a stenographer and dictated a plan of local government which I then discussed with Col. Robertson on Monday, 30 July. It met with Col. Robertson's wholehearted approval and he asked me to go out to Gorizia, after having telephoned Lt. Col. Smuts, to discuss the plan with the latter. I did so, and after conferring with Lt. Col. Smuts and Major Gold, his Legal Officer, I obtained their approval to the scheme. During my conference, I obtained information as to the present structure in Gorizia. Later in the evening, I conferred with Lt. Col. Kucera, City Commissioner for Trieste, and explained the plan to him. He said that it met all of his desires.

6. Col. Robertson said he would confer with Lt. Col. Armstrong, Area Commissioner of Trieste, and Lt. Col. Orpwood, Area Commissioner of Pola, on the plan and would inform this HQ as to the final decision. He was very anxious to get the thing adopted and, although he anticipated there would be difficulty in getting the Yugoslav element to accept it without too much insistence, he felt it was the fairest plan that could be presented.

7. *Outline of Plan of Local Government Organization for Venezia Giulia: Appendix "F".* The plan of organization and administration of local and civil government prepared by me is predicated on the fact that AMG must retain rigid control over the machinery of government and, although generally an Italian administrative structure would be set up, due recognition would have to be given to the prevalence of several ethnic groups in Venezia Giulia. The Communal and Provincial units of government are preserved, with the exception that, pursuant to action already taken by the SCAO, the so-called provinces are named areas.

Instead of the title "Prefect" that of "Area President" has been adopted and instead of "Sindaco" or "Podesta," the term "First Citizen" ("Primo Cittadino") is used. The latter title is not mine but Col. Robertson's, who feels that the Italian term of "Podesta" or "Sindaco" would not go down well in the Region.

Instead of the Giunta Provinciale Amministrativa and a Fascist Consulta, which were provided by Italian law existing on 8 September 1943 (GPA and Deputazione Provinciale provided under system we installed in Italy), provision has been made for an Area Council to act as a purely advisory body to the Area President (see Article 4). The Area President has been vested with the powers of a Prefect and Provincial and Prefectural local government bodies (see Article 2). He is empowered to create a basic Prefectural office with functionaries to whom he may delegate his powers of review and supervision of Provincial and Communal matters (see Article 3). Thus, a fundamental governmental machinery has been set up which may be organized along traditional Italian administrative lines, and yet with any variation necessitated by the local situation.

The same principles which led to the creation of a Provincial machinery dictated the organization of the Communal government (see Articles 5, 6 and 7). Article 8 was designed to enable the Trieste Area Commissioner to have 5 Communes in the Sesana area administered by as few officials as possible for purposes of economy. I have provided for the retention of the Commune as a unit and at the same time provided for the carrying out of the ordinary functions of administration for a combination of Communes by one official. This follows historic Italian precedent, incidentally.

I am not enthused about the insertion of Article 9, setting up District Committees. This was in the plan proposed by Lt. Col. Smuts, whose area is overwhelmingly Slovene, and who feels that a District system must be retained to some extent. I have modified his proposal, however, by making it quite clear that the District Committees have no supervision or control over the First Citizens or the Communal Councils. They are to be a purely advisory body to the Area President who is authorized to submit matters to them with the approval of AMG. The control of Allied Military Government over the entire civil organization is indicated in Article 10.

8. I believe that the draft of organization is inflexible enough to serve as a good basic structure of civil government. Col. Robertson expressed his gratitude for the assistance I gave and said that he would keep us informed as to developments. He expects to be in Rome about 7 August.

RRT/pec   [s]   RALPH R. TEMPLE
                  Major
                  Deputy Director
                  Local Government Sub Commission

Bibliography

Adleman, Robert H. and Col. George Walton. *Rome Fell Today*. Boston: Little, Brown, 1968; Bantam Books, 1970.

Angelicus and Ruben. (pseuds.) *Sotto Due Bandiere*. F. Zigiotti, ed. Trieste: n.p., 1948.

Bass, Robert Hugo and Elizabeth Marbury, eds. *The Soviet-Yugoslav Controversy, 1948–58: A Documentary Record*. New York: Prospect Books, 1959.

Campbell, John C., ed., *Successful Negotiation: Trieste 1954*. Princeton, N.J.: Princeton University Press, 1976.

Čermelj, Lavo. *Life and Death Struggle of a National Minority: The Jugoslavs in Italy*. Translated by F. C. Copeland. 2nd ed. Ljubljana: Tiskarna ljudske, 1945.

Churchill, Winston S. *Triumph and Tragedy*. New York: Houghton Mifflin, 1953; Bantam Books, 1962.

Coles, Harry L. and Albert K. Weinberg. *Civil Affairs Soldiers Become Governors*. Washington, D.C.: Office of the Chief of Military History, Department of the Army, 1964.

Cox, Geoffrey. *The Race for Trieste*. London: William Kimber, 1977.

———. *The Road to Trieste*. London: Heinemann, 1947.

Davenport, Marcia. *Too Strong for Fantasy*. New York: Charles Scribner's Sons, 1967.

Djilas, Milovan. *Tito: The Story from Inside*. Translated by Vasilije Kojić and Richard Hayes. New York: Harcourt Brace Jovanovich, 1980.

Eisenhower, Dwight D. *Mandate for Change, 1953–1956*. Garden City, N.Y.: Doubleday, 1963.

Friedrich, Carl J. et al. *American Experiences in Military Government in World War II*. New York: Rinehart, 1948.

Goodrich, Leland M. and Edward Hambro. *Charter of the United Nations: Commentary and Documents*. Boston: World Peace Foundation, 1949.

Halle, Louis J. *The Cold War as History*. New York: Harper & Row, 1967.

Harris, C. R. S. *Allied Military Administration of Italy, 1943–45*. London: Her Majesty's Stationery Office, 1957.

Komer, Robert W. *Civil Affairs and Military Government in the Mediterranean*

Theater. Washington, D.C.: Office of the Chief of Military History, Department of the Army, circa 1950 (restricted).

Lisiani, Vladimiro. *Goodbye Trieste* (in Italian). Milan: U. Mursia, 1964.

MacLean, Fitzroy. *Tito: The Man Who Defied Hitler and Stalin*. New York: Ballantine, 1957.

Macmillan, Harold. *Tides of Fortune*. London: Macmillan, 1969.

Nicolson, Nigel. *Alex: The Life of Field Marshal Earl Alexander of Tunis*. New York: Atheneum, 1973.

Novak, Bogdan C. *Trieste, 1941–1954*. Chicago: University of Chicago Press, 1970.

Powell, Nicolas. *Travellers to Trieste*. London: Faber and Faber, 1977.

Risolo, Michele. *Il fascismo nella Venezia Giulia: Dalle origini alla marcia su Roma*. Trieste, 1932.

Soviet-Yugoslav Controversy 1948–1958: A Documentary Record. New York: Prospect Books, 1959.

Sprigge, Sylvia. "Trieste Diary." *The World Today: Chatham House Review*, New Series 1, no. 4, October 1945.

Taylor, Henry J. *Men and Power*. New York: Dodd & Mead, 1946.

U.S. Department of State. "Recommendation for Return of Free Territory of Trieste to Italy." *Bulletin* 18, March 28, 1948.

Whiteman, Marjorie M. *Digest of International Law*, Vol. 3. Washington, D.C.: Department of State Publication 7737, 1964.

ADDENDUM

Compendia of proclamations, orders, instructions, etc., and manuals not attributable to named authors.

Allied Commission for Italy; Allied Military Government 13th Corps; Allied Military Government Venezia Giulia; Allied Military Government Free Territory of Trieste. *Allied Military Government Gazette* (proclamations, orders, etc.), Vols. I–VII, 1945–1954.

Allied Commission–Italy. *Desk Guide to Italy* (restricted), 1945.

Allied Control Commission–Italy. *Instructions for the Guidance of Officers of the Commission*, Vols. I and II, 1944.

Allied Military Government of Occupied Territory (AMGOT). *A.M.G.O.T. Plan, Proclamations and Instructions*, 1943.

British Ministry of Economic Warfare. *Italy: Zone Handbook no. 15, Venezia Giulia e Zara. Part I, People and Administration; Part II, Economic Survey; Map Section (secret) 1943–44; Part III, Local Directory and Personalities*.

U.S. Department of the Army. *Department of the Army Field Manual FM 27–5: Civil Affairs Military Government*.

U.S. War Department. *Basic Field Manual 27–10: Rules of Land Warfare*, 1944.

Chronology

February 21, 1945

Field Marshal Alexander, Supreme Allied Commander, Mediterranean Theater of Operations meets Marshal Tito of Yugoslavia in Belgrade to discuss the Trieste question.

April 29, 1945

Surrender agreement for all German troops in Italy is signed.

April 30, 1945

A Partisan detachment of the Yugoslav Ninth Corps enters Trieste.

May 1, 1945

Units of Yugoslav Fourth Army enter Trieste.

May 2, 1945

Units of Second New Zealand Division enter Trieste.

May 2, 1945

German troops in Italy surrender per agreement.

May 3, 1945

German troops in Trieste surrender to New Zealanders.

June 12, 1945

Allied Military Government activated in Zone A of Venezia Giulia.

August 11, 1945

General Order No. 11 establishes local government plan (Zone A).

August 18, 1945

Proclamation No. 5 dissolves fascist organizations and repeals laws favoring fascism.

September 15, 1945

Council of Foreign Ministers, in London, begins consideration of the Trieste problem.

March 9–April 5, 1946

Council of Foreign Ministers' Commission of Experts (delegates from the United States, USSR, France, and Great Britain) visits Venezia Giulia.

July 3, 1946

Council of Foreign Ministers, at Paris peace conference, announces proposed terms of Peace Treaty with Italy, including establishment of the Free Territory of Trieste.

September 28, 1946

Territorial Commission of the peace conference adopts the proposal of the Council of Foreign Ministers.

October 9–10, 1946

A plenary session of the peace conference adopts the proposal of the Council of Foreign Ministers.

November 28, 1946

Council of Foreign Ministers approves the treaty of peace, the new boundaries, and the statute of the Free Territory of Trieste.

January 5, 1947–February 27, 1947

Financial Commission of the Council of Foreign Ministers visits the Free Territory of Trieste.

January 10, 1947

U.N. Security Council guarantees the independence of the Free Territory of Trieste.

February 10, 1947

Free Territory of Trieste formalized in the Italian peace treaty signed in Paris.

March 7, 1947–September 5, 1947

Boundary Commission draws new frontiers between Italy, Yugoslavia, and the Free Territory of Trieste (commonly known as the French Line).

September 15, 1947

Free Territory of Trieste comes into being under the terms of the Italian peace treaty, and the occupation of Venezia Giulia Zone A by British and U.S. forces ends. (R Day).

March 20, 1948

Tripartite proposal by the United States, Great Britain, and France recommends that the Free Territory of Trieste be returned to Italy.

June 25, 1948

Order 259 creates a new form of local government on the pattern of the Italian system.

October 15, 1948

British-U.S. Zone, Free Territory of Trieste, is admitted as a participating country in the European Recovery Program with the signing of the bilateral agreement between the United States and the zone commander acting for the Zone.

October 5, 1954

U.N. Security Council confers on Italy and Yugoslavia the temporary right, without sovereignty, to conduct the civil administration in the west and east zones into which the Free Territory had been divided since 1947.

November 10, 1975

Agreement between the governments of Italy and Yugoslavia converts into a permanent international boundary (with a few minor changes) the line between the zones that had been administered by Italy and Yugoslavia, respectively, since 1954.

Index

Action Party, 24
Alexander, Field Marshal Harold, 19, 26, 35, 75, 77, 84, 117; and Tito, 36, 39–40, 41, 66; proclamations of, 77, 102; evaluation of, 78–79; and opposition to General Order No. 11, 94; Bowman communicates ideas on Venezia Giulia to, 98–99, 105
Allied Commission (Rome), 11, 17, 25, 66, 76, 93, 99, 108, 128
Allied Force Headquarters (AFH), 59, 93, 116, 133
Allied Information Service, 134
Allied Military Government (AMG), 62, 115, 151; treatment of, in Trieste press, 90; military rule under, 94, 96; teachers hired by, 97–98; Bowman's comments on, 139–40. *See also* Military government
Allied Psychological Warfare Board (PWB), 90, 134
American Red Cross, 18, 21, 124
Anderson, Rosemary, 112
Armstrong, Lt. Col., 159, 160
Ascoli, Graziado, 2, 3
Assicurazioni Generali, 3, 47
Atlee, Clement, 53, 95
Austria, 3, 9, 12, 72, 105
Austro-Hungarian empire, 2, 3, 4, 33–34, 129
Avvogadro, Giancarlo, 104

Banks, Monte, 72
Barbana (Italy), 122–23

Belgrade Agreement, 41–42
Bell for Adano, A, 122–23
Benson, Group Capt. C. E., 11, 12
Bevin, Ernest, 53, 73, 109
Black Brigade, 20
Blackley, Travers, 67–68
Blatnik, Capt. John, 59–60
Bologna, 14, 25, 27, 29, 105; captured by Allies, 19; military government in, 19–22
Bora winds, 50–51, 65, 128
Boundary Commission, 105–11 *passim*
Bowman, Alfred Connor, 29–30, 159; regional command in Emilia-Romagna, 13, 15–22; honors accorded, 28–29, 105; scope of responsibility in Trieste, 43–44, 103; directs repairs of war damage, 53–54, 123–25; visits Yugoslav authorities, 59–60; daily routine, 66–74, 122–25, 134; personal background, 67, 136; rumors of mistresses, 70, 71, 80–82; place in military command structure, 75–76; and local and international press, 82–90 *passim*, 136, 137–39; background knowledge of Trieste, 84–85; on free state status for Venezia Giulia, 99; home leave of, 105, 106; and governorship of free territory, 131; departure from Trieste, 136–42; visit to Czechoslovakia, 143–49
Boy Scouts: in Trieste, 60–61

Index

Bradley, Gen. Omar, 137
Bretto di Sopra (Italy), 124

Caccia, Harold, 25
Caleidoscopio, 83, 116–17, 135
Cammarata, Angelo E., 134–35
Caprini, Fanny, 132
Carr, Brig. John Matthew, 16
Cemeteries: in Trieste, 121
Charles, Sir Noel, 98
Christian-Democrat Party, 24
Churches: in Trieste, 46
Churchill, Randolph, 86
Churchill, Winston S., 39, 40, 53, 113; Iron Curtain speech, 6, 41, 107
Cianfarra, Camille, 86
Cittadella, La, 83, 136, 137
Civilians: and military government, 8–9
Clark, Gen. Mark, 16, 72
Clayton, Will, 146, 148
Cleveland, Harlan, 25
Cold War, 6–7
Cole, Bill, 123
Committee of Liberation, Slovene, 91–92, 95, 98
Communists: Italian, 24, 25, 94–95; Slovene, 96
Corriere Di Trieste, Il, 90
Councils of National Liberation, Italian, 37
Courts: in Trieste, 102–3
Cox, Sir Geoffrey, 38
Crittenberger, Gen. Willis D., 16
Croats, 4, 32, 34, 36, 94–95, 106–7
Czechoslovakia, 143–49

Dabney, Virginius, 117
D'Annunzio, Gabriele, 4–5
Davenport, Marcia, 150
D-Day Dodgers, 14
Defascism, 102–3
Demonstrations: in Trieste, 47–50, 65, 106–8, 112, 128, 135, 141

Deportees, 54–57
De Winton, Robin, 126, 129–31
Difesa Popolare (People's Defense), 61, 92
Dozza, Guiseppe, 25, 29, 105
Duino Agreement, 41, 58, 91
Duke, Doris, 86
Dulles, John Foster, 154
Dunlop, Brig. John K., 16, 78

Economic Commission, 128, 132
Edelman, Maurice, 86
Edinost (Unity), 34
Education: in Venezia Giulia, 27, 77–78, 97–98
Eighth Army, British, 11, 12, 39
Eighty-eighth American Infantry Division ("Blue Devils"), 104–5, 114–15, 124, 137
Eisenhower, Gen. Dwight D., 116, 136–37, 154
Emilia-Romagna region, 10, 12, 13, 24–25, 29–30
Epuration, 103–4

Fields, Gracie, 72
Fifth Army, U.S., 11, 12, 28
Fiske, Col. Norman, 132
Fiume (Rijeka), 4–5, 34, 60, 84
Florence, 16, 28, 47, 132
Foiba, 37, 55–56
Foreign ministers meeting, Allied, 99, 101, 110
Fourth Army, Yugoslav, 31, 35–40 *passim*
France, 3, 4, 26; in Allied Military Government, 9; policy on Trieste, 110, 120, 153–54
Freese, Duane, 17
Freyberg, Gen. Bernard, 40
Frieden, Cy, 85, 86
Fronte dell' Indipendenza, 118

Garibaldini (communist) partisans, 24, 33

General Order No. 7, 103–4
General Order No. 11, 93–96, 98
Gerashcenko (Soviet delegate to Trieste), 106
Germany, 9, 124, 147; occupation of Venezia Giulia, 3, 5; troops surrender in Trieste, 36, 37, 40, 109
Giornale Alleato, 90
Giornale di Trieste, 138
Giro d'Italia, 112
Glas Zaveznikov, 90
Gold, Major, 159, 160
Gorizia (Görz), 4, 36, 44, 57, 106, 113, 124; General Order No. 11 in, 93, 96; epuration in, 104; local government of, 159, 160
Gorizia Gap, 44
Gottwald, Klement, 144, 149
Governorship of Free Territory of Trieste, 116–18, 152–54
Great Britain, 4, 25, 53, 70–71, 100, 152; role in military government, 9–10, 11–12, 16, 68; plans for Venezia Giulia, 109, 110, 153–54
Gruenther, Gen. Alfred M., 16

Hamblen, Gen. Arch, 41, 107
Hamburger, Phil, 85
Hapsburg empire, 3, 157–58. *See also* Austro-Hungarian empire
Harding of Petherton, Lord, 53, 63, 108, 131, 132, 137, 138; and establishment of Venezia Giulia police force, 61; role as Bowman's superior, 77–78, 105, 135; view of Bowman's activities, 115, 117
Hartley, Hubert Horton-Smith, 17
Hersey, John, 122, 123
Herter, Christian, 152
Holjevac (Yugoslav colonel), 60
Hull, Cordell, 113

Hume, Brig. Gen. Edgar Erskine, 11

International Rules of Land Warfare, 67
Interpreters, 88–89
Irredentism, 2–3, 4, 16, 32, 130–31
Irredentist Party, 130
Istrian Peninsula, 3, 57, 113, 129
Italian Red Cross, 57, 121
Italy, 110, 157; irredentism of, 2–3, 130–31; contests Yugoslavia for Venezia Giulia, 4–5, 105; nature of military government in, 9–10, 11–12; geographic division of, for military government, 10–11; Soviet policy on claims to Venezia Giulia of, 105, 109; Yugoslav Treaty of Peace with, 129, 132, 151; resolution of Trieste issue and, 153–55

Joint Economic Commission (Allies-Yugoslavia), 58–59
Jovanović (Yugoslav general), 41
Joyce, Stanislaus, 88–89

Koreman, Sidney, 86
Kucera, Lt. Gen. Henry P., 43, 159, 160
Kuchel, Sen. Thomas H., 154

La Guardia, Fiorello, 114–17 *passim*
Lavoratore, Il, 90, 112, 138
Lee, Gen. John C. H. ("Court House"), 75, 106, 122, 131, 132
Liberal Party, 24

McCormick, Anne O'Hare, 86
McGurn, Barrett, 86
Macmillan, Harold, 17, 18–19, 78, 108

Mandic, Mrs. (alleged mistress), 80
Maria (alleged mistress), 81
Marriages of U.S./British enlisted men, 135
Marshall, George C., 144, 149
Marshall, Col. Robert, 15
Marshall Plan, 148, 149, 152; Paris conference, 144–49 *passim*
Masaryk, Jan, 144, 145–50, 153
Masaryk, Thomas, 146
Mathews, Herbert, 86
Mauldin, Bill, 85
Memorandum of Agreement of Free Territory of Trieste, 154, 155
Military government, 7–8; civilians under, 8–9; personnel of, 9; integrated nature of, 9–10, 67–69, 75–76, 78–79; U.S. school of, 11, 67–68, 84; composition of regional teams in Italy, 11–12; in Emilia-Romagna region, 15–22, 27–28, 30–31; terms of, in Belgrade Agreement documents, 41–42; scope of Bowman's jurisdiction, and problems faced, 43–44, 52–65, 76–77; government functions and local government organization, 76–77, 159–61; and General Order No. 11, 93–96, 98; loss of U.S. administrators, 102; defascism and epuration by, 102–4; history of, 121–22; town reconstruction by, 123–26; winding down of, 128, 133
Miramare Castle (Trieste), 44–45
Monfalcone (Italy), 95, 122, 125
Monfort, Col. Nelson, 66, 69
Montgomery, Field Marshal Bernard L., 72, 122
Moore, Maj. Gen. Bryant, 114, 115, 132
Moorhead, Alan, 122

Morgan, Lt. Gen. Sir William D., 40–41, 58, 76
Morgan-Jovanović Agreement, 41, 58
Morgan Line, 40–41, 42, 58, 59, 76, 107, 129
Murrow, Edward R., 72
Museums and galleries: in Trieste, 46–47
Mussolini, Benito, 10, 11, 18, 29, 97

National Committees of Liberation (Italian), 24, 25, 26
National Committees of Liberation (Yugoslav), 33, 91–92, 95, 98
New Zealand: troops in Trieste, 31–40 *passim*, 109
Nixon, Richard M., 152
Noel-Baker, Philip, 100

Oberdan, Guglielmo, 130
Orpwood, Lt. Col., 159, 160
Osimo Agreement, 155, 156

Papal Relief, 57
Partisans (guerrillas), 23–27, 31, 33; surrender of weapons, 26–27; communist preponderance among, 24–25; occupation of Trieste, 36–38
Pasquinelli, Maria, 126, 129–31, 151
Patton, Gen. George, 44
Penrith, Elizabeth, 112
People's Court (Trieste), 92
Petacci, Clara, 29
Piccolo, Il, 34
Plebescite: for Trieste, 109
Plezzo (Italy), 124
Pola (Pula), 36, 53, 57, 129, 132, 159; opposes General Order No. 11, 93, 94–95; exodus of Italians from, 120–21

Index   173

Poletti, Col. Charles, 15, 89
Police: in Venezia Giulia, 61–65, 105, 106–7, 131, 135
Polish Corps (British Eighth Army), 20
Port facilities: in Trieste, 4, 47, 53
Press: Bowman's relations with local journalists, 82–84, 136–39; Bowman's relations with American and international journalists, 85–90, 108; inaccuracies in, 87–88; Trieste newspapers, 90; on defascism, 103; on choice of governor, 116–17
Primorski Dnevnik, 90, 138–39

Rapallo, Treaty of (1920), 4, 32, 34
Reakes, Major, 160
Refugee camps, 57
Reston, James "Scotty," 86, 117
Riccione (Italy), 17
Richardson, Maj. Gerry, 63, 64
Ridgway, Gen. Matthew, 75
Rijeka (Yugoslavia), 4–5. *See also* Fiume
Robertson, Col., 105, 106, 159, 160, 161
Robertson, Gen. Sir Brian, 78
Rome: Allied Commission in, 12, 16, 17
Rome, Treaty of (1924), 5
Roosevelt, Franklin D., 17, 39
Royal (British) Engineers, 116

St. Germain, Treaty of (1919), 4, 5
San Giusto, Castle of (Trieste), 45–46
San Marino, Republic of, 15–16
Santin, Msgr. Antonio, 117, 123
Sauro, Guglielmo, 130
Schnabl family, 69
Scouting, 60–61
"Scrounging," 17–18

Shipping industry: in Trieste, 3, 4, 47
Slovene National Home (*Narodni Dom*), 34, 35
Slovene National Liberation Front, 33
Slovene Regional Council, 36
Slovenes, 4, 32–35, 54, 62, 81–83, 112; Slovene-language schools, 97–98; in Venezia Giulia police force, 106–7
Slovenia, 36
Smuts, Lt. Col., 159, 160, 161
Socialist Party, 24
Stalin, Joseph V., 26–27, 110, 113, 149
Steinhardt, Laurence, 145, 146
Stettinus, Edward, 111, 146
Stone, Admiral Ellery W., 11, 66, 76
Street, Col. Douglas M., 90
Strikes, 104, 114, 155–16
Sullivan, William, 112
Sulzberger, C. L., 86

Teheran Conference, 113
Temple, Maj. Ralph R., 93, 159–61
Territorial Commission of Appeal, 104
Theaters: in Trieste, 46
Thirteenth Corps, British, 115
Thirteenth Infantry Brigade, British, 129
Tito, Josip Broz, 19, 44, 57, 84, 95, 106, 115, 157; Fourth Army of, 31, 35–38, 39–40; discussions with Allies on postwar terms, 36, 40, 41; and Yugoslav claims in Venezia Giulia, 107, 113; rumor of coup by, 108–9
Treaty of Peace (Allies-Italy), 151–54 *passim*
Trieste, 1, 6, 7; history of, 3–5, 32, 34; physical and economic

Trieste (*continued*)
  characteristics of, 3–4, 44–51 *passim*; ethnic composition, 4, 32, 34, 90, 97–98, 129; Yugoslav goals in, and occupation by Tito, 31–32, 35–38, 91–93, 107–9, 113; Allied disposition of in 1945, 39–42; AMG jurisdiction, and problems of military government in, 43–44, 52–65; demonstrations in, 47–50, 106–7, 112; police in, 61–65, 92; journalistic interest in, 85–90; population opposes General Order No. 11, 93–95; and free territory idea, 99–100, 118; defascism and epuration in, 102–4; major powers' positions on, 105, 111, 153–54; arrival of American families, 119–20; exodus of Pola Italians to, 121; fate of, in postwar decades, 151–58; contemporary life in, 156–58; local government in, 159–61
Trieste, Free Territory of, 99–100, 110, 111, 129; governorship of, 116–18; flag for, 123; transitory statute on administration, 151–52; proposal for cession to Italy, 153–54; Memorandum of Agreement on (1954), 154; Osimo Agreement on, 155–56
Trieste, University of, 77, 83, 105, 134–35
Trieste United States Troops (TRUST), 45
Truman, Harry S, 39–40, 73, 95, 123, 127

Union of Soviet Socialist Republics, 6–7, 53, 59, 107, 157; and disarming of Italian Partisans, 26–27; positions on Trieste, 105, 109–10, 120, 153

United Nations, 42, 101, 111, 156; and Free Territory of Trieste, 99, 110, 155–58; Security Council, 111, 116, 151–58 *passim*
United Nations Relief and Rehabilitation Administration (UNRRA), 114, 115, 143, 148
United States, 6, 7, 70–71, 111, 152; support for Italian leftists by, 23–24, 25; and Trieste border plans, 110, 153–54; conditions in 1947, 127

Venezia Giulia, 19, 84, 104; description and history, 1–3, 4, 5, 34–35; Italian and Yugoslav claims to, 4–5, 33, 36, 91–93; AMG in, 12, 40–42, 123–26, 159–61; *foiba* tradition in, 55–56; organization of police in, 61–65, 106–7, 131, 135; bilingual educational problem in, 97–98; plan for free state in, 99, 101, 110, 116–17, 120; defascism and epuration in, 102–4; territorial division of, 110, 120; town reconstruction in, 123–26; report on local government organization in, 159–61
Villa Ina *or* Schnabl (Trieste), 69–70
Voce Libera, La, 90

Weeber, Capt. Richard, 44
Wellard, James, 86
White, Geoffrey, 61
World War I, 4–5, 34, 44, 130

Young Fascists, 60
Yugoslav Army of National Liberation, 33
Yugoslavia, 4, 31, 53, 110, 113, 115–16, 139, 149; claims to Venezia Giulia by, 3, 4–5; occu-

pies part of Venezia Giulia, 40–41, 54–57, 91–93, 152; rumors of coup in Trieste by, 108–9; rebuilding of villages by AMG in, 125–26; signs Treaty of Peace with Italy, 129; incorporates part of Free Territory of Trieste, 153, 154, 155; contemporary use of Trieste by residents of, 156–58; ethnic composition of, 157

Yugoslav National Council, 36

Yugoslav National Liberation Committee, 33, 91–92, 95, 98

About the Author

Colonel Bowman was educated in the Detroit public schools, Wayne State University, and the University of Michigan. Following two years of law practice in Detroit, he moved to California, where he practiced law during the 1930s as house counsel for a corporation, deputy city attorney of Los Angeles, and associate in a major law firm. He opened his own law office in 1938, having meanwhile also become an officer in the Army Reserve.

He was called to active duty immediately following the Japanese attack on Pearl Harbor. In early 1943, he was ordered to the School of Military Government and then to North Africa and Italy where he served for four years in a variety of critical military government positions. In 1944–45, he headed the Allied Military Government in the Pisa-Rimini combat zone, and in 1945–1947 directed the British-American postwar trusteeship in the Trieste area.

In later years, as a regular army officer, he conducted the first statutory codification of all the laws relating to the armed forces, served as chief of the army's Military Government and Claims Divisions, and rounded out his military career as First Army staff judge advocate. In late 1950, when the United Nations appeared to be winning the Korean War, he was dispatched to the Far East to establish a United Nations Military Government in North Korea, an assignment that was terminated by the Chinese incursion. Three years later he served as head of the Negotiations Committee for the United Nations Component of the Military Armistice Commission. As chief of claims he had the special and extraordinary responsibility of settling the many thousands of claims authorized by a compassionate statute after the Texas City disaster of 1947.

Since his retirement from the army and ensuing participation as a civilian in an in-depth study of Soviet space capabilities for the Defense Department, he has devoted himself to extensive world travel and to writing on legal, historical, and political subjects for professional publications and the press.